CONTENTS

THOUGHT IS DEAD
MOVING BEYOND SPIRITUAL MATERIALISM

As long as you are in conflict with yourselves it is not possible for you to be in harmony with this society around you.

U.G. Krishnamurti

Chapter One

SPIRITUAL GREED

Greed. You preach against greed. I'm sorry to point out this to you, because you give discourses on how to be free from greed. Are you free from greed? No. Do you want to be free from greed?

Q: No. [Laughter]

U.G.: No. Why the hell are you asking me to begin with? I am sorry to spotlight you and put you in that spotlight. So you tell me. I don't know if there is any such thing as greed. If there is a greed it is operating here in this moment in you. I don't like to use that word bastard, but you are the greediest bastard in this moment. I am using this only to drive it home for you.

So you think that I have *something*, which you want. If there is money you can rob a bank and take the money. There is something there. But here, it is your *assumption* that I have something, that I am functioning differently, that I am this, that and the other. You want to be like me. If that is not greed, what else is it? She is laughing.

Q: She knows I'm greedy. [Laughter]

U.G.: When are you going to be free from greed? When are you going to say, "I'm the greediest man"? Right? When are you going to be free from greed? When? Tell me.

Q: Tomorrow.

U.G.: It is in operation here! The solution for that greed, if at all you are interested in freeing yourself from greed, is to allow that greed to fill the whole of your being. Every cell in your body, everything in that body should vibrate with that greed. By wanting to be free from greed, for whatever reason you want to be free from greed, you are destroying the possibility of freeing yourself from greed.

Through greed you'll be free from greed. Are you ready to accept it? It is the selfishness that will free you from selfishness, and not the preaching or practice of selflessness.

Chapter Two

SPIRITUAL CONMEN

U.G.: Those Zen bastards! They institutionalized meditation. Jokers! I was never attracted to Zen masters. Never! Because they were all the followers of Buddha and what Buddhism tried to preach to the world. So reject it. You all are them! They institutionalized the whole thing. They invented the techniques of meditation.

Q: The Hindus say that the Upanishads are much superior.

U.G.: Who? They have to because they are Indian.

Q: At least the Upanishads have not institutionalized those things.

U.G.: They created these metaphysics, the intellectuals. And what you find in the Upanishads is not the people whom they are talking about, but the aspirations of those people who *want* to be in that state. That's why Buddha had too much intellectual nonsense. That fellow didn't have the guts, sir, to go to the end. And when he had this experience he said, as long as there is a single soul imprisoned in the veil of illusion I refuse to enter the gates of Nirvana. He never entered the gates of Nirvana—he refused. For the sake of mankind; like the politicians talking of mankind, humanity, you know? And then for the first time in the history of mankind he introduced the element of conversion, proselytization. He created a Sangha—he moved from place to place, followed by all these people, and he wouldn't allow women to join his order for a long time. There were a lot of protestations. Finally he relented and admitted them also. Then came along—this is my reading of the history, take it or leave it—an Ashoka, the King, and he used that as an instrument of power, very forcibly in this country.

But then Jainism spread in the South, not Buddhism. That's why you have so many Jain temples. The place where I grew up is called "The place of temples". Not Buddhist temples, but Jain monasteries. A lot of prostitutes lived there; along with of course...they go together: prostitutes and spiritual teachers. It is not a religion.

Q: But what is the story that he refused to enter paradise?

U.G.: Who?

Q: Buddha.

U.G.: He didn't have the guts. He stopped with some petty little mystical experience, like anybody else. Like all these gurus you have in the marketplace. Even Ramana Maharishi stopped there. All of them. That prevents the possibility of these people coming out with something original. So they have to rely upon the authority of the scriptures, and then they interpret. How can a fellow that has written four volumes talk of enlightenment? Tell me. And claim that he is an enlightened man? He cannot do that. It's a sales speech. They sell that stuff to the poor people. There is authority for them. The filthy word you are using—enlightenment. Sorry, sir.

Q: Buddha had authority?

U.G.: No, no, not at all. It was all political, the man, the King Ashoka. Otherwise, Buddhism, Christianity, Islam would have remained small cults. They became the instruments of power. They forced...of course, they didn't use violence here in this country, but when Buddhism spread to Japan, particularly, the monasteries maintained armies—trained armies—and supplied them to the rival kings. That's a trait of holiness.

Sannyasins never existed in India. It is difficult to understand because you are all Sannyasins. [Laughter] Because you've made a business out of that.

Q: Do you say that Buddha is not at all original?

U.G.: Not at all. He pretended like J. Krishnamurti—original—by not using any authority that existed before. Because that is what the Upanishads said: it is an authority of its own. So I am *"pramanaya"*, I think. Why should I quote that nonsense? I must wash my mouth. [Laughter]

Q: Buddha is very original.

U.G.: It is all intellectual nonsense. Not original, all saints do that, what did he do? No, sir. The monasteries supplied armies to the rival kings. The founder of Zen, the first fellow who went there, Boddhidarma, called Buddha a barbarian, and said that Buddhist teachings are nothing but toilet paper. He had the guts to say that in the 7th century! He is quoted there.

Q: The emperor asked him, what is the holy teaching of the Buddha? And he said, no holiness, just...

U.G.: Kill him, he said. If you meet Buddha kill him. Well, anyway, why do you need a Buddha? It's the same as Christianity, the conversion—with violence! You may say that Buddhism is not violent—Indians are cowards. You swallow anything! Hinduism is not a religion at all like Judaism. It's social, political, economic; a lot of things put together. It's just a way of life and a way of thinking, nothing else. That is culture. It is not art, beauty, poetry, music—that is not culture. So that is part of your thinking.

You think that you are superior to me because you are a swami. What have you renounced? You have not renounced anything. And the second thing is, they pick up a new job, a new language, use that and feel great. That's all. Use those words, Krishnamurtian lingo.

"A truly religious person does not want anything for himself [laughter], but it is the responsibility of you all [laughter] to see that my teaching is *the* teaching, and should be preserved for posterity in its pristine purity. So give liberally to my cause." [Laughter]

Q: He uttered that?

U.G.: Sure, he said "cause". You see, he was brought up in poor conditions. He didn't have anything in his life. Here it is the other way around. Buddha was born as a king. Anything I wanted I could have had. Anything, anything in the world, I had as a matter of fact, everything that one could reasonably ask for. If I wanted to buy a Rolls-Royce car, just in a jiffy…by writing a check on the Imperial Bank of India I could buy, so you see. Money was not, in that sense, a primary preoccupation. That is not my interest.

See, I knew how you could make money. If I dedicated myself to money I would have been the world's richest man—world's richest! All the billionaires in America would be insignificant. That was not my interest. My only interest was to be certain that Buddha was a conman.

These people around you, the claimants, are not really the genuine people. There is a dichotomy in their lives—what they said and what they were in actual life, in reality. It intrigued me. I didn't call them dishonest people or any such thing. So if the teaching produced me it doesn't help me in any way. The teacher must be wrong. You usually don't blame the teachers—you exonerate them. The teacher is not responsible for that you have not done it enough; you have not done things in the right way, so you exonerate the teacher. I was not interested in that.

If that teaching runs counter to the way I am functioning, then something's wrong. You know? If I am not jealous, something wrong with me. I am full of jealousy, I am full of greed. And you are talking of a state that doesn't exist at all. You claim that you are in that state; I don't see that you are operating that way. I am very close to them. As I said, I was always surrounded by such people. I lived in the company of sages, saints, saviors of mankind, or so they claimed to be...

Murderers, rapists, conmen, thieves, everybody, any day. I offer their company and not the spiritual people. There is some sort of integrity in them. You know exactly what they want, and they don't mince matters.

Q: There are degrees.

U.G.: No degree. I never accepted one of degree. No, if you say one of degree you have destroyed the possibility of going to the end. Degree never interested me.

Q: For all these examinations you have to study hard...

U.G.: That's a different matter. You don't know how to operate that camera—through a repetitive process you learn how to operate it. You improve it, you modify it. That is how the whole technology came into existence. This I discovered when I was very young. So if thought is the instrument to put me in a thoughtless state I am not interested in that at all. This cannot be the instrument, you know? How can this be the instrument? So the teachers are false. These are all the claimants. You must go to the source.

Q: Everybody was caught up in that game, that in the process of evolution, thinking…

U.G.: Evolution doesn't exist. There may not be any such thing as evolution. You can throw out all evolution, much less in the field of spirituality. There you can see it creates a hierarchical structure. "I am far superior to others" they say. First you become disciple, this, that, 2nd degree, 3rd degree, then you become an Arhat. What nonsense are these Arhats? You know? They fight amongst themselves.

Q: How do you free yourself from that kind of conditioning?

U.G.: What? Don't use that word conditioning! What do you mean by conditioning? What exactly do you mean by conditioning?

Q: Because everybody everywhere we see that this continuous process of living is there.

U.G.: But you don't understand the basic thing that this is also conditioning you in a different way.

Q: Which one?

U.G.: Whatever you are doing to uncondition yourself is conditioning you in a different way. So that is not important for me—whether you are conditioning the ancient way, modern way, or Krishnamurtian way. You may talk of unconditioned mind, but he doesn't operate like a man living in a state of unconditioned mind. So if you talk of the experience of silent mind, what is he talking about? How can you experience a silent mind, and then describe that as love, beatitude, immensity? I'm not at all interested in that. And then why do you describe that as love, beatitude, immensity? That is the sales speech. That is what you are interested in. So he's selling you that. He has created just a structure of thought—nothing else is there. So you reject. You know? You go to the source.

They themselves are conmen—con themselves and con the whole of mankind. Then the next question is: why do I con myself? All of them are conmen—not one single exception. Those who were there before me, those who are there with me today, around me, and the teachers yet to be born—they will be conmen.

Q: That means they con themselves. They fool themselves that they are going somewhere, reaching somewhere.

U.G.: They say that they have come into a state—whatever it is, unconditioned mind, you know? "A transformed individual." There is nothing here to be transformed. Why the hell are you talking about radical transformation, radical mutation? Why the hell are you talking about it? Why? I asked him these questions. He didn't have any answers—he was giving the answers of a politician: neither confirm nor deny. I am not interested in that. I would have asked Ramana Maharishi also: "Did you, by posing this question to yourself—Who am I?—get into that enlightened state?"

I asked J. Krishnamurti: "You are taking all these people on a bogus chartered flight. You got into that state of a transformed individual through this step-by-step, logically?" No, he said.

"Then why the hell are you talking about it?" I asked.

"If it works, it works. If it doesn't, it doesn't," he told me. That joker. You will find all that in his teachings. Whatever was convenient, he put it in that book. That's all. Anything that anybody said against him, or attacking him…

Q: Because he believed.

U.G.: I tell you, he never freed himself from the world teacher business. Never. Why he dissolved that was because of the family quarrel amongst themselves. That is one thing. The money remained with him.

I asked him also: "Why is the money sitting there in the Dutch bank?"

Then he said, "What do you want me to do? How do I invite all these people that contributed this money? There is no way I can return it."

He returned only that castle. I didn't see that castle. First time, this year, when I was there, we were passing through that place, and so I asked them, "Take me to that castle." Now it is not in the family. They sold it to some school.

What was I saying? He said, "If it works, it works. If it doesn't, it doesn't work." What the hell are you doing?! What for? Huh? What for? Ah…The world teacher business…then he wanted to be on his own and build himself up into a spiritual teacher on his own, which he succeeded.

And there was a time when he was using only mystical language, until he was struck in California during the war. He was not allowed to talk, and he was in the company of Aldous Huxley and that joker, I forget his name. They were meeting every day. They had nothing else to do. He was growing potatoes or tomatoes, and roses. So he had a chance to discuss with all those people. Then he created a lingo, which I call Krishnamurtian lingo. In 1942, I think, he met a few people in one of the farms there in the Midwest. That was the first time he used that lingo. Before that, he was using "I am my beloved"—all that nonsense. "Immortal friend." Even in 1932, because my English was not good enough to understand, but even now my English is not good. So, I heard him, first time in 1928, in that nations school, as a boy. Even in 1928 I was only 10 years old.

He was a student in that national college there, started by Annie Besant. They wanted to show that the Theosophical Society is not in any way involved with J. Krishnamurti. That was a show, you see. That's it.

Then the question arises: why are you conning yourself? Why are you fooling yourself? Why can't you reject the totality of human thought? Not one. We are all the variations of the same. So there was no answer to that question and even as a little boy—everything I want, everything, my tastes, my appreciation of beauty, everything, everything is what they wanted me to have.

What I learned about sex was from my servants, not from these saints. Some strange things started in me. Not that I wanted to f___ [laughter]. No, not in that sense. That was the beginning of my questioning. "Why this celibacy? Why this nonsense?" Like that. I learned a lot. I learned everything not from spiritual teachers and not from secular teachers, but in my own way. Of course, if I want to learn how to operate that camera I have to learn from him, and he learned from somebody else. So through a repetitive process you learn. That's the only instrument we have. It cannot conceive of the possibility except in time. It has taken so many years for you to become an engineer; it has taken me so many years for me to be somebody in this world. There is no other way. Everything that I want, all my tastes, all my dislikes, all my belief. What they wanted me to want. So I wanted something else, something that was different from that. Even as a little boy I didn't want that. Why were they forcing me to want this one and not that one? But it never occurred to me that this is also a want.

Q: To want something which nobody else wanted.

U.G.: It's also a want. Like this thought: why the hell do you want to be in a thoughtless state? What am I using? I am using my thoughts, and these are not my thoughts, those jokers have put these thoughts in me. Where are my thoughts? You know?

Q: You were feeling that way?

U.G.: Yes, in the very beginning.

Q: You were seeing your thoughts?

U.G.: No, I didn't see any thoughts. I didn't see any thinker. I didn't see any thinking there.

Q: How could you say these are *not* my thoughts? These *are* my thoughts.

U.G.: What I see is only about thought, but not thought. Even today, what do you see? C'mon. How do you find out? Why are you asking these idiotic questions about thought? "What is thought?" How do you go about it? What do you see there? How do you separate yourself from what you call thought and look at it? Actually you don't look at thought. There is no thought about thought. What they said about it—thought is matter, thought is this, thought is that, that's all you see there, but not thought. After all, you see, what is thought? Noise. Sound. Thought is sound.

Chapter Three

THE TRANSLATING CAMERA

U.G.: Not through intellect, not through listening. That joker talked for years and years on the art of listening, art of seeing—that bastard J. Krishnamurti. Not through listening, not through intellect. You can buy those people with Rolls-Royce cars or even Mercedes-Benz cars. You know? No, not through sacrifice. There is nothing to sacrifice. Sannyasins[1] are out! And these are the things that you are trying to use to attain that must be dropped, must be sacrificed. The very idea of renouncing something must be given up. That is that.

It cannot be passed on from somebody to the other. So there is no succession there. No Pontiffs coming after that. So it finishes with this fellow. The whole organizations, ashrams, are brothels.

Q: Obviously this person [pointing to U.G.], whatever he speaks, it has some kind of vitality, some kind of energy. Which can be used…

---

[1] The sannyasi lives a celibate life without possessions, practises yoga meditation—or in other traditions, bhakti, or devotional meditation, with prayers to their chosen deity or God.

U.G.: No, it cannot be used.

Q: But that energy, if it has got energy, can be used to…

U.G.: No, it cannot be used because the instrument which you have is your thought, that dare not touch this life. So it destroys that. You play with that game. It dare not touch life. It is not interested in that at all. The energy which you are talking about is the thought-induced energy. That is what you experience. *This* can never be experienced, can never be touched by dead thought. *This* is something living.

Q: No, what I make out of you has a vitality. This can be used by me!

U.G.: This has the freshness of the living quality, not interpretation, not memorized things. Just like that flower. If you use that simile it is mystifying. It's not interested in you looking at the flower. Why the hell do you want to tell the people to look at the flower? It's not even conscious of the fact that it's a beautiful flower! Why? If you call that a beautiful flower and look at it, it is a sensual activity. That's all. And so that is what these people exploit. Sensuality! Nothing else! All your spiritual experiences—bliss, beatitude, love—how can that be love? There must be two. So love is out. Such a man will never talk of love. Your bastard guru, what happened to his unconditioned love? That bastard. When he said I'm cursing him he will be down in the garbage. You know? Your guru sent a special message to you.

Q: Yeah.

U.G.: What happened to that unconditional love? They just talk, those bastards, on the platform and fool you. Nothing else. And you are fooled. There he is—he has an unconditioned love. What nonsense it is! How can such a man curse you? "I'm going to destroy him." Where are you? You are on the top, that bastard is somewhere reduced to ashes. People can go there and worship him. No. See what happened?

Q: But can one use you for purposes….you know, for…?

U.G.: You can use some phrases but there is no teaching here. No teaching. You cannot create any systematic thought out of this! Anybody who has tried who is competent to do this has admitted that there is nothing that they can do. You can use the phrases. I'm telling you, don't use a source, you're original.

Q: Your perceptions can be used, and one feels very…

U.G.: Sorry, no.

Q: …light, by using your perceptions.

U.G.: You don't use high-sounding words! This perception will destroy the perceiver—there. So you cannot…

Q: U.G., am I like a parrot?

U.G.: You are worse. The guru doesn't admit that he is a parrot. They do not admit that they are just parrots. They pretend that they are not. They are something else.

What is U.G.? He is a useless guy, he keeps repeating.

Mr. M., you haven't got a chance. This is not what you are interested in. You cannot be interested in this. How can you be interested in this? You tell me. That phoney-baloney that they are preaching on the platforms.

Q: By wanting to record this it means that I don't have a chance.

U.G.: You don't have a chance.

Q: This instrument used to record you....

U.G.: That is quite different. It is more interesting than you. You are translating, filtering. The camera is just recording. It is not involved in what it is recording.

Q: So we never see things as they are?

U.G.: Exactly the way they are? Never. You can't.

Q: We only see things as *we* are?

U.G.: No. As you *want* to. That's all.

Q: So is there a difference in me looking at you, and this camera looking at you?

U.G.: No, no difference. That is more faithful than you are. It is just recording. It doesn't even know that it is recording. And if you play, it comes out exactly that way that it is recorded. That's all. You are translating, interpreting it. You see? Otherwise you are not there. Finished.

Chapter Four

FIRST AND LAST PUBLIC TALK

Let me, at the very outset, thank the authorities of the Indian Institute of World Culture for giving me this opportunity to meet you all here. I was very reluctant to accept the invitation of Mr. Venkataramaiah. But somehow, if I may use that word, I was trapped into this kind of a thing.

As Mr. Kothari pointed out, I don't like to give talks at all. You all seem to be very fond of listening to speeches, talks, lectures, discussions, discourses, conversations, and so on. I do not know if at any time you realize for yourself and by yourself that you never listen to anybody or anything in this world. You always listen to yourself. I really don't know what to say. I don't know what you want to listen to and what I am expected to do.

This is supposed to be a discourse and a dialogue. I very often point out to those who come to see me and talk things over that no dialogue is possible and no dialogue is necessary. It may sound very strange to you, but, nevertheless, the fact does remain that no dialogue is possible and yet no dialogue is necessary.

If you will permit me, I will say a few words, to set the ball rolling, as it were. That's a very hackneyed and over-worked expression, but that would serve our purpose.

I am going to say a few words about the state of not knowing. How can anybody say anything about the 'state of not knowing?' I have necessarily to use words. Can we use words without indulging in abstract concepts. I say we can. But I do not, at the same time, mean that it is a non-verbal conceptualization. That is a funny thing—there is no such thing as non-verbal conceptualization at all. But, perhaps, a few words like this will enable you to understand [that] the methods of thought prevent you from understanding the limitations of thought as a means to directly experience life and its movements.

This 'state of not knowing' is not [just] my particular state. (This I call it a 'Natural State' of your being.) This is as much your natural state as it is mine. It is not the state of a God-realized man; it is not the state of a Self-realized man. It is not the state of a holy man. It is the natural state of every one of you here. But since you are looking to somebody else and you are reaching out for some kind of a state of liberation, freedom, or moksha—I don't know what words you want to use—you are lost.

But, how can one understand the limitations of thought? Naturally, the only instrument we have is the instrument of thought. But what is thought? I can give you a lot of definitions, and you know a lot of definitions about thought. I can say that thought is just matter; thought is vibration; and we are all functioning in this sphere of thought. And we pick up these thoughts because this human organism is an electro-magnetic field. And this electro-magnetic field is the product of culture. It may sound very inappropriate on this occasion to say that in order to be in your natural state, all that man has thought and felt before you must be swept aside and must be brushed aside. And that means the culture in which you are brought up must go down the drain or out of the window. Is it possible? It is possible. But, at the same time, it is so difficult, because you are the product of that culture and you are that. You are not different from that. You cannot separate yourself from that culture. And yet, this culture is the stumbling block for us to be in our natural state.

Can this 'Natural State' be captured, contained and expressed through words? It cannot. It is not a conscious state of your existence. It can never become part of your conscious thinking. And then why do I talk of this state of not knowing? For all practical purposes it does not exist at all. It can never become part of your conscious thinking.

Here, I have to explain what I mean by the word 'consciousness'. You and I mean two different things, probably—I don't know. When do you become conscious of a thing? Only when the thought comes in between what is there in front of you and what is supposed to be there inside of you. That is consciousness. So, you have to necessarily use thought to become conscious of the things around you, or the persons around you. Otherwise, you are not conscious of the things at all. And, at the same time, you are not unconscious. But there is an area where you are neither conscious nor unconscious. But that 'consciousness'—if I may use that word—expresses itself in its own way; and what prevents that consciousness to express itself in its own way is the movement of thought.

What can anyone do about this thought? It has a tremendous momentum of millions and millions of years. Can I do anything about that thought? Can I stop it? Can I mold it? Can I shape it? Can I do anything about it? But yet, our culture, our civilization, our education—all these have forced us to use that instrument to get something for us. So, can that instrument be used to understand its own nature? It is not possible. And yet, when you see the tremendous nature of this movement of thought, and that there isn't anything that you can do about it, it naturally slows down and falls in its natural pattern.

When I say that, I do not, of course, mean what these people in India talk about—that thought must be used in order to get into a thoughtless state or into a meditative state. But there is no such thing as a thoughtless state at all. Thoughts are there; they will be there all the time. Thoughts will disappear only when you become a dead corpse—let me use these two words—'dead corpse'. Otherwise, thoughts are there and they are going to be there. If all the religious teachers tell us that you are going into a 'thoughtless state,' they are taking us all for a ride. They can promise you that in that thoughtless state—in that state of silence, in that state of quietness, or in that state of a 'Quiet Mind,' or whatever phrase you want to use—there will be this real 'bliss,' 'beatitude,' 'love,' 'religious joy,' and 'ecstatic state of being'. All that is balderdash. Because, that state—if there is any state like the state of bliss—it can never become part of your consciousness. It can never become part of your conscious existence.

So, you might as well throw the whole thing—the whole crap of these ideas, concepts and abstractions about the blissful states—into a cocked hat, if I may use that American slang.

So, what is one to do? Can anybody help you? No outside agency can help you. That means a complete and total rejection, as I said in the beginning, of all that man has thought and felt before you. As long as there is any trace of knowledge, in any shape, in any form, in your consciousness, you are living in a divided state of consciousness.

He [Mr. Kothari] referred to my coming into a state of 'not knowing' or 'the calamity,' as I myself refer to that. What happened? I don't know. Suddenly thought has fallen into its natural state. The continuity has come to an end. So, what I am saying is not the product of thinking. It is not manufactured by my thought structure inside. Nor is it a logically ascertained premise. But what is happening here is only the expression of that state of being where you do not know what is happening. You do not know how this organism is functioning. As he [Mr. Kothari] himself referred to, this is a pure and simple physical and physiological state of being. It has no religious undertones or overtones. It has no mystical content whatsoever. And, at the same time, this extraordinary thing, the extraordinary intelligence that is there, which is a product of centuries of human evolution, is able to express itself and deal with any problem and any situation without creating problems for us.

Question: May I interrupt you? I was told by people who are around you that when this calamity befell you, you couldn't recognize even ordinary things. You were asking like a newborn child, "What is this?" Even if there was a flower in front of you, you did not know if that was a flower. Then you would ask, "What is this?" And the Swiss lady who was keeping house for you, who was looking after you, Valentine, [she is here with us], said "This is a flower." Then you would ask again, "What is this?" You mean to say that at the time when the calamity took place, all recognition was gone?

U.G.: Not only then, but even now, as I said, this is a state of 'not knowing'. Since the memory is there in the background, it begins to operate when there is a demand for it. That demand is created by an outside agency, because there is no entity here. There is no center here. There is no self here. There is no Atman [the immortal self or soul] here. There is no soul here at all. You may not agree. You may not accept it, but that unfortunately happens to be a fact. The totality of thoughts and feelings is not there. But [in you] there is an illusion that there is a totality of your feelings and thoughts. This human organism is responding to the challenges from outside. You are functioning in the sphere—so, thousands and thousands, perhaps millions and millions of sensations are bombarding this body. Since there is no center here, since there is no mind here, since there is nothing here, what is it that is happening? What is happening here [is that] this human organism is responding to the challenges, or to the stimuli, if I may put it that way.

So, there is nobody here who is translating these sensations in terms of past experiences. But there is a living contact with the things around. That is all that is there. One sensation after another is hitting this organism. And at the same time there is no coordinator here. This state of not knowing is not in relationship to your Brahman, or your Nirguna Brahman or Saguna Brahman [Brahman is the Transcendent Absolute, non-dual One, beyond apprehension or comprehension] or any such thing. This state of not knowing is in its relationship to the things that are there around you. You may be looking at a flower. You may think that it is a crazy state. Perhaps it is—I don't know. You do not know what you are looking at. But when there is a demand for that—and that demand always comes from outside, [asking] what is that, and then the knowledge, the information that is there, locked up in this organism comes and says that it is a rose, that this is a microphone, that's a man, that's a woman, and so on and so forth. This is not because there is a drive from inside, but the outside challenge brings out this answer. So, I say that this action is always taking place outside of this organism, not inside.

How do I know that these sensations are bombarding or hitting this organism all the time? It is only because there is a consciousness which is conscious of itself and there is nobody who is conscious of the things that are happening. This is a living organism and that living state is functioning in its own way, in its natural way.

Mr. Kothari: U.G., it appears to me this Nirguna Brahman, Atman, whatever it is—when somebody uses the word Bhuma [absolute consciousness], another uses the word "unknown," the third man says "akal" [the timeless], the fourth one says something else—all of them say that this cannot be described, "Neti, Neti" ["Not this, not this"]. Probably they meant the same thing; I don't know. I think they meant probably what you are saying as "totality." As I understand it, Brahman means "totality." If I would translate this state into terms of those times, probably it is the same thing as being in the state of Brahman and [it is] thought which is limiting the "alpa", which is limiting the "bhuma", which is limiting the limitless, since it does not function like that, creating an individuality within you. Maybe I am wrong, maybe I am translating, but I say that it is possible that the person who listens to you doesn't know the old terms. You are not going to use the old terms, because the new terms are your terms. And every teacher, every person who has come into some state like this has generally used a different term, a different word, according to his background. But personally I think you mean the same thing. This is a commentary on what you are saying.

U.G.: What do you want me to say? [Laughter] If they have understood what there is, they wouldn't be here. They wouldn't go to anybody. They wouldn't ask these questions at all. If they translate what I am saying, in terms of their particular fancy or their particular background, that's their tragedy; it would be their misery. It hasn't helped them. This is my question: Has it helped you? Why are you hung up on these phrases? They are after all phrases. When once you realize, when once this is understood—how this mechanism is operating, how automatic it is, how mechanical it is, you will realize that all these phrases have no meaning at all. You may very well ask me why I am using these phrases: [it is] because you and I have created this unfortunate situation where you have put me here on the dais and asked me to talk, and naturally, as I said in the beginning, I have to use words. So, the moment I stop talking, the whole thing has come to a stop inside. Is that so? It is so here [in my case], because there is no continuity of thought.

We go back to the thing he [Mr. Kothari] referred to, about the things around me. Here there is a table. I don't know what it is. And, at the same time, if you ask me, "What is that?" I would immediately say, "It's a chair." It [the knowledge] is there in the background. It comes automatically, like an arrow. But otherwise, this [the impression I have] is just a reflection of this [the thing in front of me]. I don't translate this as "bimbavatu [like an image]" at all. But I have to use that word: this is reflecting the thing exactly the way it is. I don't want to use these metaphysical phrases because you will immediately translate them in terms of your particular parallel. There is no subject here independent of the object at all. So, there is nothing here [inside of me]. What is there is all that is there, and you do not know what it is. So, now you turn there, and this object has just disappeared, there is something else. This has completely and totally disappeared from here and then what is there is a thing that is there in front of me and it is just like this object, exactly the way it is. But you do not know what it is. That is why I say it is a state of not knowing. Probably you will find parallels to these things. What I am trying to point out is the absence of what you are all doing at this moment; [that] is the state that I am describing, and it is not [just] my state [but] that is the way you are [also] functioning.

May I give an example of what is happening in the field of spectroscopy. I don't read books, but sometimes I read magazines. I get interested in these things. They have developed very powerful lenses to take photos of objects. They have developed micro-seconds, nanoseconds and picoseconds. It doesn't mean anything to you and me—it's all technical language. Now they are able to take pictures of objects, say for instance, of this table, every pico second. Every picture is different. In exactly the same way, the reflection of that object is once now; another time, you turn this side, you are back again—it's again you. But don't translate this in terms of newness and oldness. It cannot be communicated to you at all. This can never become part of your experiencing structure.

I am throwing a lot of conclusions at you. But even a thing like this cannot be experienced by you at all. I don't know if you understand this. You have necessarily to abstract this in order to experience a thing. So, what I am trying to say is that you can never experience your own natural state. This can never become part of your experiencing structure. And what you are all trying to do all the time is to make that—whatever you want—to realize or discover— part of this experiencing structure. So your experiencing structure and your natural state cannot co-exist at the same time.

Mr. Kothari: The way you want to say is that everything is in a continuous flux all the time. The human eye being limited and the human ear being limited, and the human senses being limited, [they] cannot respond to the quick movement of existence. They don't respond, they don't reflect. You say, unless there is a need of recognition, this thought, this verbalization, this word—it is just a way of affecting the life within you, and that's all. There is no need to verbalize, or translate, if possible. Am I describing what I understand of your state?

U.G.: That's what you understand. [Laughter] [I am not trying to be irreverent.]

Mr. Kothari: [I am Neither.] What happens is, it seems to me ... [is he trying to mislead you by saying?...] that all these persons coming to this have tried to express this in terms of what somebody else has said. It is all the time new. It is all the time fresh. It is all the time indescribably beautiful. When they came into the world they have to say [something about it]. He says it is neither new nor old. It is never old. It is never old because he does not take [it] into the [past] experience. It is not translated, unless, as he says, it is needed for translation. Otherwise, every time, life is indescribably, extraordinarily—all that is outside—is extraordinarily fresh, extraordinarily new, though he doesn't use the words 'fresh' and 'new'. This is how I understand.

U.G.: This I must stress: that the need for the operation of thought, or the movements of thought to come into being, is decided by factors outside of this organism. When and why and how this translation is to come into being is decided by an action outside. The actions are always taking place outside. When there is a demand, the movement of thought probably separates itself for a while to meet the demands of the situation and then it is back again in the movement of life. So, thought is only functional in value, and it has no other value at all.

What is more is that the continuity of thought is destroying the sensitivity of your senses. When the movement of thought is not continuous, the senses begin to function in an extraordinarily sensitive way. When I use the word sensitivity, I mean the sensitivity of the senses and not the sensitivity of the mind. The sensitivity of the mind is a trick of your mind, and you can create a state of mind where you feel sensitive to the feelings of everybody, to the things around you and wallow in that sickly state of mind and think you are getting somewhere. This is a thing that is there [you are doing this] all the time.

There is nothing to achieve, there is nothing to accomplish, nothing to attain, and no destination to arrive at. And what prevents what is there, this living state, from expressing itself in its own way is the movement of thought which is there only for the purposes of functioning in this world. When the movement of thought is not there—I have to use the clauses in terms of time—but time is thought. When thought is there, time is there. When thought is there, sex is there, when thought is there, God is there. When thought is not there, there is no God, there is no sex, nothing is there. It may sound objectionable to you to accept my statement [Mr. Kothari:" Not at all."], but the drug of virtues you practice, the practice of virtues is not a foundation for it at all. And the practice of abstinence, continence, and celibacy is not the path to it. But if you want to indulge in them and feel greatly superior, it's your own business. I am not here to reform you. I am not here to lead you anywhere. But this is a fact. You have to understand a fact as a fact. It is not a logically ascertained thing, it is not a rational thing [so as] to understand it rationally. A fact is a movement. Truth is movement. Reality is movement. But I don't want to use these words, because they are all loaded words. You know all about them. The unfortunate thing about the whole business is that you know a lot about these things, and that is the misery of you all. This is a thing which you do not know at all. I am not claiming that I know it. I myself don't know. That is why I say I don't know. It's a state of not knowing. Let alone God, let alone reality, ultimate or otherwise, I don't know what I am looking at—the very person who has been with me all the time, day and night. That is my situation. If I tell this to a psychiatrist, he will probably put me on a couch and say something is radically wrong with me. Probably, I am functioning like any other human being. He doesn't understand that. That's his problem, it is not my problem anymore. So, all your search—for truth, God, Reality—you use any phrase you like, is a false thing. You are all on a merry-go-round, and you want to go round and round and round.

How can you ask for a thing which you do not know? How can you search for a thing which you do not know? You all seem to know. You have an image of this state. From the description of this state probably you have already created [an image]. What state? Somebody asked me: "What is the state you are in?" "What State? Mysore State or Tamil Nadu State? What state are you talking about?" [Mysore and Tamil Nadu are geographical regions in India] This is my response. What is the state you are talking about? This is your natural state. You don't want to understand that. You don't want to be in your natural state. It requires an extraordinary intelligence to be in your natural state, to be yourself.

You always want to be somebody else; you want to imitate the life of somebody else—you want to imitate the life of Jesus, you want to imitate the life of Buddha, you want to imitate the life of Shankara. You can't do it, because you don't know what is there behind. You will end up changing your robes, from rose to saffron, saffron to yellow, or from yellow to rose, depending upon your particular fancy. How can you ask for a thing which you do not know? How can you search for a thing which you do not know? That is my question. So, search has no meaning at all. Only when the search comes to an end, what there is will express itself, in its own way. You cannot tamper with that. You cannot manipulate that. You cannot manipulate the action of the thing which is there, which has an extraordinary intelligence.

To be yourself is the easiest thing. And you don't want to be in your state. You'd rather be somebody else, imitate the life of somebody else. That's your problem. To be yourself doesn't need any time at all. But you talk of timelessness, which is a mockery. To be yourself, do you need time? To be a good man, to be a marvelously religious man, to be in a state of peace, to be in a state bliss, naturally you need time. That will always be tomorrow. When tomorrow arrives, you say, "All right, day after tomorrow." That is time. [I am] Not [talking about] this metaphysical or philosophical thing. I am not talking about metaphysical time and timeless. There is no such thing as the timeless.

I am making assertions, statements and conclusions—you will object to them. Take it or leave it. I don't expect you to accept anything that I am saying. You are not in a position to accept or reject it. You can reject it because it does not fit into the particular framework of your philosophy—Shankara, Gaudapada, Ramanuja, Madhvacharya, God knows what—we have too many of them here. So how can you understand this? The only thing to do is to throw in the towel. Turn your back on the whole business. That is why, it takes extraordinary courage, not the courage or the bravado of these people who climb Mount Everest or try to swim across the English Channel, or cross the Pacific or Atlantic—whatever their fancy—on a raft. That is not what I mean. What I mean is the courage. You quote your Bhagavad Gita, or your Brahma Sutras, "kaschid dhirah." All these phrases. What do they mean? "Abhayam Brahma." [Fearless is Brahman.] Why do you all repeat these phrases? It has no meaning. It's a mechanical thing. "How are you?" "I am all right, I am fine. Just fine. I couldn't be better." In America, you know, [they say] "How are you this morning," "I am just fine. I couldn't be better." In exactly the same way, you throw these phrases at everybody. If you understand the way this mechanical structure is functioning inside of you, you see the absurdity of the whole business of discussing these matters everlastingly. Can you throw the whole business out of the window and walk out?

[**Mr. Kothari**]: I think what he means is... When I meet him.... I have known him for about five years now. And I am many times reminded, on account of my having read the Upanishads and this and that... I am reminded of [the passage in] the Isavasyopanishad, "asmai nayatu patha," "Oh fire, takes us on the right path!" I find there is a sort fire in him which sometimes, I fear, would frighten a person who does not understand, quite grasp, even intellectually, what he is trying to convey. As I understand it, he is not advocating anything. His whole approach is.... He has no system. He says something about these states—that this is your natural state. But the whole thing, this achievement business, to get something, [the state being] like something, comparing something to some imaginary state which one has formulated, an image we got by reading about those things—that he says is all futile. It is strengthening the mental structure, it is strengthening the thought structure, and it is giving a life to it—which, he says, is all useless. It is the cause of your very misery, all the problems. It seems he has seen it himself. And the structure went phut, the whole thing broke inside, and, as he says, he even does not know [it himself]. That is the state of unknowing. When he says this, I am reminded of the words of Jnaneswar who says, "I don't know what I am or where I am." Even avidya [ignorance] has gone, and vidya [knowledge] has gone also. So, I see

... only I want to remind some of my listeners here ... that the newness of expression, whatever he is trying to convey, is as old as the hills and as fresh as the vibrations from that thing now. It is as fresh or even fresher than the words I am speaking, the sounds that I am throwing at you. It is more fresh than that. It is sanatana [ancient] and puratana [old]. But, he says, it requires total courage.

Another thing that I have noticed in him is a kind of—I am talking personally about you, but, as there is no personality, it doesn't matter. [Laughter]—a tremendous, fearlessness, "abhayam tattva samsuptih." I would again quote the Gita, the daivika sampatti [the divine qualities], this is something that does not happen in the usual, normal men in whom the animal fear is functioning all the time, as he says. But he does not come out of that [state]. I don't know how he came to it. But [there is in him] a tremendous fearlessness and a sense of abandonment. He is not a perfect specimen of all the wonderful virtues. He gets annoyed, and he gets angry also. For a moment you see the cloud of anger on his face, and after a minute you see the full moon is again on his face, smiling. The clouds have disappeared all of a sudden. So, I say, he says there is no risk in the matter. Probably, in whatever he conveys, there is some suggestion. He says you don't have the courage to throw in the towel. You don't have the fearlessness. "[inaudible] ... have got to go." He says, "You throw out the speaker also." I hope some of you certainly have got the hang of what he is trying to convey.

Q: [Inaudible]

[**Mr. Kothari**]: Your question is, when there is hunger and pain in the body, what happens? You mean what happens to him or what happens to you?

U.G.: I will tell you. First of all, there is no hunger at all, in the sense in which we use the word. It's pure and simple chemistry. And then there is what you call hunger which is like any other sensation, you understand. The consciousness or life, or whatever you want to call it, becomes conscious of that thing [called hunger]. And [the next moment] it is gone. It is not there. It does not push you to reach out for food. And so, the next sensation is coming. It's a continuous movement. You are looking at something and this is finished. Probably your body will become weaker and weaker, if you don't eat food. People give me food; so I eat food. Otherwise, there is no such thing as hunger at all. And the pain, there is physical pain. Since there is no continuity of thought, as I pointed out, there is no continuity of pain. It comes in impulses like that—just the way you are throwing out words. There is no continuity of the pain. I don't want to use the word psychological pain, because it gets us involved in..., because we will begin to tie things in knots. There is only physical pain and there is no other pain. But even that physical pain is not continuous, and so it is not much of a pain, in the sense in which we use the word.

Q: What is the way or method of getting into this state?

U.G.: What state? When the movement in the direction of wanting to be into your own natural state or in the state of God knows whom you want to be, your idol, or your hero or your master [is there]—it is there—this movement in any direction, is taking you away from yourself. That is all that I am pointing out. When the movement is not there, you are your natural state. So, the sadhana, the method, or system, or the technique, is taking you away from yourself in the direction of the state you want to be in and that is the state of somebody else. As I pointed out, you have the knowledge about this state. Unfortunately, so many people have talked about it. I am already doing mischief, perhaps. Kick them all out, on their backs. [Mr. Kothari: "Not now!"—Laughter] Yes, throw stones at me and walk out. [Mr. Kothari: "They don't have any."] My interest is to send you packing, as the expression has it. If you can do that, you will never go to listen to anybody. [Someone in the audience: "If I throw stones, I will go to jail."] I will not take you to jail. That's a problem with the society in which you are caught. I can't help you. I will not be the first one to complain about it.... Are you not tired? I can go on. That's enough, I suppose.

I haven't said anything. What all you think I have said is a 'bag'. You think it makes sense. How can it make sense? If you think that it makes sense, you haven't understood a thing. If you think that it doesn't make any sense, you haven't understood it either. It's just words—[you are] listening to this noise—words, words, words—mechanically coming out of this organism. I don't know how they are coming. I wish I knew. I wish I knew how I got into ... what state? It always irritates me when people ask me "You tell us something ...." About what state? What state are you talking about? I know Mysore. I am in the Mysore State. How do I know that I am in the Mysore State? Because people tell me that I am in Mysore. So, what state you want to get into? That is your natural state, I am saying.

What takes you away from your state is this movement in the direction of wanting to be in some state other than yourself. To be yourself doesn't need time. If I am a village idiot, I remain a village idiot. Finish. I don't want to be an intelligent man. Even if my neighbor takes advantage of his extraordinary intelligence and exploits [me], good luck. What can I do? To accept the reality, this is the reality of the world. There is no other world. There is no other reality, ultimate reality. This is the only reality. You have to function in this world. You can't run away from this world. How can you run away from this world? Because you are that world. Where you can you go? Hide yourself in a cave? Yes, you are taking your thoughts wherever you go. You cannot run away from your shadow. It's there all the time. So, you can't do a thing about thought. That's all that I am saying. When you realize the absurdity of all your effort to do something about the thought—it's creating the problem; it's misery for you; you can't do anything—when you can't do anything, when you realize that you can't do a thing about it, it's not there. You are not using it [thought] as a means to get something for you.

I want to say this again. You desire. If you do not want anything, there is no thought at all. You understand? Wanting is thinking, it doesn't matter what you want—want self-realization, want God- realization—you want anything, that means you have to use this instrument. These are not your thoughts, these are not your feelings. You may not like it. They belong to somebody else. You want to make them your own. You have unfortunately made them your own. That's why you ask all these questions. Why do you ask all these questions? These questions have been put before to so many people—all the sages, saints and saviors of mankind, the holy men dead and alive. They are all ready to answer. They have composed a lot of lullabies. You go and listen to them and go to sleep, if you want to. That's what you are interested in. You want somebody else to pat on your back and say, "Oh, fine, just fine, you are doing very well. Do more and more of the same and you will reach the destination you want to arrive at." What is the destination you want to arrive at? To be gentle, meek, to be soft, to talk and whisper. You know if you go to some of these monasteries in the West, the Trappist, they talk and whisper. They don't even understand what the other man is saying. That's the secret to the spiritual path.

Mr. Kothari: When a man is in love, he talks and whispers to his beloved. What objection do you have to anybody talking and whispering?

U.G.: I have no objection at all. I wonder if he is really in love. [Laughter] You don't even have to talk about it. You want to reassure your partner that you are in love with that person. It isn't worth a tinker's damn, that love. That's not love at all. You can call it love. I don't want to go into that. It's a forbidden subject. They ask me, "Do you have anything to say about ....?" It's a four letter word. It's like any other word—'dog', 'pig', 'love'. In love, can there be any relationship at all? Can you have any relationship? This is your problem. You are all the time trying to have relationship with people. You cannot have any relationship with people at all. "Love is relationship." "Life is relationship." All that guff. Trite. Crap. You memorize and repeat them [those phrases]. They all become fancy phrases these days. "Freedom," "first and last freedom," and "the freedoms that come in between." What is this nonsense? This is like any other trite [phrase], any other crap that these people are repeating. You have memorized a new set of phrases. That's all you are doing. You sit and discuss everlastingly all this awareness. What is that awareness you are talking about? How can you be aware of this? Can you at any time be aware of it? If you are aware of this once in your lifetime, the whole structure has collapsed; it has fallen in its proper place. You don't have to do a thing about it. So, it doesn't mean a thing at all. You can talk of awareness—choiceless or otherwise—or conditioning. Conditioning—what can you do about it? Conditioning is intelligence. You can't do a damn thing about it. You can't free yourself [from it]. If you want to free yourself from your conditioning, or uncondition yourself and all that nonsense that is going on…. How are you going to uncondition yourself? You create another conditioning—instead of repeating Upanishads you will repeat some other thing, the fancy books.

Q: What is the secret of total happiness?

U.G.: There is no happiness. I never ask myself the question. So many people ask me that question: "Are you happy?" What is that question? Funny question. I never ask [myself] that question, "Am I happy?" Total happiness is an invention. [Mr. Kothari: "Invention of the mind, you mean?"] There is no mind. Where is the mind? Is the mind separate from the body? Distinguished from the body? Apart from the body? These questions have no meaning at all. You have no way of separating yourself from what is going on. The moment you separate yourself means you have a knowledge about it—the knowledge given by either the biologists, the physiologists, the psychologists or the religious people. So through that you are looking at it. You cannot experience anything without knowledge. You cannot experience this at all, let alone Brahman or reality. You cannot experience this at all. Only through an abstraction. And what is that abstraction? The knowledge you have about it. This has been put there. Your mother told you, or your neighbor or friend told you that this is a table. What the hell is that, you don't know, apart from what you have been told. Every time you look at this, you have to repeat to yourself that it is a table. What are you doing that for? This is my question. This is the continuity I am talking about. You want to reassure yourself that you are there. The "I" is nothing but this word. There is no "I" independent of this word. Maybe you find some parallel [to what I am saying] in Shankara or God knows what. [Mr. Kothari:] Plenty, plenty. Because this is the same thing that they have talked about.

Q: [Inaudible] ...thoughtless state as in "this, this, this."

U.G.: Yes, yes. They called it 'cit'. "The consciousness I am talking about, is a state where there is no division which says that you are asleep, that you are awake, that you are dreaming .... There is no division at all. I don't even know if I am alive or dead. This is my state. I have no way of knowing for myself. The doctor can come and say that I want to examine your lung, your lung is functioning all right—there is heartbeat, there is this, that and the other—you are alive. That's all right. I am delighted. You reassure me that I am a living being. But...

Q: How do you know at any time that you are in the Natural State?

U.G.: That, as I said, can never become part of your conscious existence. It begins to express itself. The expression of that is energy; and that is action. It is acting all the time. This is not a mystical term. What I mean by action is [that] the action is taking place always outside. The senses are working at their peak capacity all the time. It's not because you want to look at a particular thing. There is no time even for the eyelids to blink for a second. They have to stay open all the time. And when they are tired, it [the body] has its own naturally built-in mechanism, which cuts off the sensation. And then it's back again.

Q: What is that mechanism?

U.G.: What is that mechanism? Supposing somebody gives you an answer. So, where are you? Can you separate yourself from that mechanism? This is what I am saying. You can separate yourself from the mechanism and look at it only through the knowledge, whether the knowledge is provided by a physician or by a saint or by a sage. And that [knowledge] is worthless. Because you are projecting this knowledge on what you are looking at, and that knowledge is creating or producing these experiences. That can never become part of that experiencing structure. That's the trouble. You want to experience this. You can't experience this at all. Whether it is the consciousness that I am talking of, or the living state or the state of not knowing or the things that are there around [you]. How is it expressing itself? It is expressing itself as energy, it is expressing itself as action, in its own way. If I use some words, "It is aware of itself, it is aware of its own its incredible death, it is conscious of itself;"—all these phrases may sound very mystical to you—but you cannot [experience it]. The brain physiologists, if I may quote somebody,— they are trying to understand the brain. And they have to find some means to define [it]. They have defined the brain as an instrument with which we think. They are not so sure. You cannot separate yourself from the brain and its activity and look at the brain. Can you look at your back and tell me something about your back. Somebody else must come and tell you. And he has his own ideas, fancy ideas. "You have a straight back." The doctor always observes people. And from his point of view, he would say that that man is sick, this man's back is not correct, and so forth. Or, if I see a painter, his description is something else. So, this is a thing which you cannot communicate to somebody else. Can you communicate your sex experience to somebody else? [Mr. Kothari: "Why sex experience, any experience."] Or any experience, for that matter. That's what everybody is trying to do—a painter, a poet or a writer. He is trying to communicate some experience, which he calls extraordinary experience, through his medium—writing poetry, culture. He is like any other artisan.

Q: How do you reconcile your existence with the world?

U.G.: I don't bother. Do I exist in this world? Does the world exist for me? Where is the world? I am not trying to be clever with all these phrases. I don't know a thing about it. Am I talking, am I saying anything? This is like the howling of a jackal, barking of a dog or the braying of an ass. If you can put this on that level and just listen to this vibration, you are out, you will walk out, and you will never listen to anybody in your lifetime. Finish. It doesn't have to be the talk of a self-realized man. You will realize that there is no self to realize. That's all. There is no center there. It is working in an extraordinary way.

Q: In the extinction of sense organs ..., if the sense organs do not function at all, for instance, there is death; there is a state of not knowing and you still function.

U.G.: There is no death. You are never born. You are not born at all. [Laughter] I am not trying to mystify. Because life has no beginning, it has no end. Has it a beginning, has it an end? What creates the beginning is your thought. Why are you concerned about death? There is no such as death at all. Your birth and your death can never become part of that experiencing structure. If you want to experience death, you are not going to be there. [Laughter] Somebody else will be there. It will be somebody else's misery.

Chapter Five

THE DEAD CANNOT TOUCH THE LIVING

U.G.: You see nothing! You can't listen, you don't talk about that nonsense! You see nothing there! You don't even see *this*. *This* will finish you!

Q: Well I see...

U.G.: You see nothing! Empty words you are repeating, memorized, reactive phrases and words. That's all that you are doing. Whatever is put in, like a tape recorder, you are repeating everything that is put in there, that's all. See that! How can you see? You have never seen anything in your life. I tell you, never! Probably as a baby, I don't even know that. You have never seen anything in your life. It's not in your interest to see. That knowledge will come to an end if, as you say, "I see".

Q: What am I supposed to do?

U.G.: That question...go to a teacher, he tells you? "What you should do?" You have come to the wrong man. We have been told what to do all our lives. Why do you want me to tell you what man should do? Why? Why? You tell me.

Q: It's part of our tradition to wonder what would happen if we go astray.

U.G.: Have you gone astray? You are only a frightened chicken there. You haven't even done that. You go astray and you will be surprised. You are not even going astray! You are sitting and telling me that if I don't do this I will go astray. You will be surprised that there is no going astray. Something else is happening there. There is some action there going astray—you will discover something there. But here you are sitting: "I'm afraid I'll go astray." You are not going to go astray.

Q: We are seeing people go astray...

U.G.: No! Don't bother about them. You tell me about you. Others, don't bother. It's easy for us to...

Q: Do you know how it feels like to commit suicide then?

U.G.: In that you will not understand them. Because that will never be understood for you. Whether you commit suicide or die a natural death.

Q: So we must become totally helpless?

U.G.: Why do you say that?

Q #2: Because it's in the book.

U.G.: "We must become totally helpless." You are not a helpless man. You still think that you can help yourself. You wouldn't even say that—I am totally helpless—those phrases wouldn't even arise there inside. You will never tell yourself that I am helpless.

Thank you sir. Good night. You come always towards the end.

Ah well, what shall I say then?

But you are still recording.

Q #2: I just started. I just read your book that you…

U.G.: Forget that book.

Q #2: No, I just want to…

U.G.: All that book is full of false statements, lies. It doesn't matter whether they were made by me or someone else. It doesn't matter. It's all dead. Dead things cannot touch anything living. You get this and get this straight. Nothing. Every word is dead. Every memory is dead, so it cannot touch anything living there. If it touches, the whole thing is burned, you see? It's like the live wire. All the words and phrases are just gloss, you don't play with that kind of a thing. That's why no books help us, no teachers help us, nobody can help us. And then you don't need any help. It is they who are making us help us.

Q: Do not we have anything to do?

U.G.: What do you mean—anything to do? What are you doing sir anyway? What are you doing? You are just sitting and talking.

Q: I wonder if I'm going astray…

U.G.: Go astray and you find out! You are frightened to go astray. You see someone else going astray. But what's wrong with going astray? Tell me.

Q: The people who like drugs, they become addicts. They die, they are harmful.

U.G.: Yeah, meditation is harmful according to me. Yoga is harmful. Health food is harmful. You want statistical evidence because you are a doctor? I don't eat any vitamins. I drink 1 pint of cream every day—solid cream. I'm not recommending this food to everybody. I'm not a vegetarian, I don't eat vegetables or fruit. So what's wrong? The nutritionists can talk what they want to talk. It's habit that you have to keep eating all the time. You are eating ideas. You are putting ideas into your stomach, but not food. Anything you put there, it takes care. You can laugh when I say that. Today is enough exercise for this body for one week. Why are you laughing?

Q: In that interview with that parapsychologist you mentioned something about the left body and the right body.

U.G.: One day we will probably have to find a way of treating the left body and the right body. I don't even know what I said.

Q: Do you think it has anything to do with the left brain and the right brain?

U.G.: I think that theory is already outdated. You will be surprised that the brain plays a very limited role in the functioning of this body. I don't know where or what that intelligence is. I'm not competent enough to talk about it. But there is no way you can...the physiologist may study the brain and come out with the theories of all and every kind. I don't know if the body can survive without the brain.

Q: No. Biologically, not.

U.G.: Biologically not. I agree. A fellow used to be in the marketplace here that had no legs, no hands, no eyes, nothing. Only the torso. It's amazing how the body can survive without all those things. I have known people who survived without a stomach. You can take the brain for some time and put it in a glass jar and put it back. Maybe, I don't know.

Q: You can with heart for that matter.

U.G.: Yes. Mechanically we can. We don't want to accept the fact that this is just a machine. You know? Mechanical. Everything there is mechanical. You don't want to accept for the simple reason that we have been brainwashed for centuries to believe that it is just not a machine. It is just a machine! An extraordinary machine, an extraordinary robot.

Q: How does it lubricate?

U.G.: It is self-lubricating. You don't need doctors. If something wrong with my eyes I will come to you anyways. I don't know. I don't see any special charm in putting up with any physical pain, you see? Not even for spiritual reasons. I don't see any reason why you should bear any pain to prove that you can bear pain. No. If there is somewhere that you can get the relief, go ahead and do it. One aspirin is enough, they have ten different kinds in the market. That's all a commercial business they're doing. But I don't believe in bearing pain, enduring pain, either for spiritual reason or for self-centered reasons that you can bear pain. We don't know whether that joker actually underwent the operation without anesthesia. There are some people who can bear pain...you don't have to be a spiritual man. Whether you can you withdraw everything I don't know. I haven't been impressed by one example. So we don't have any statistical evidence to prove that the fellow recovered his eye after the doctors...you were saying that or was it somebody else?

I don't know if I accept anything unless it is statistically proved. I said this also many times on television. Take, for example, God. Apart from your belief or concept of God, if—I am using *if* for the purposes of an argument—if it is proven beyond a shadow of doubt that there is no such thing as God, no religious man will stop believing in God. But if a scientist finds that there is God they will certainly believe it. Even believe in God—if it is proven. There is no question of proving the existence of God at all because it doesn't exist, you see? If I say that I am an atheist or some such thing...man created God. This way, not the other way around. You can experience any damn thing you want, create God, and put him out there and touch and feel. Take walks with God, do what you like.

God is the ultimate pleasure. Moksha, liberation, freedom, transformation, radical transformation.

Q: Sometimes your God also is a… [inaudible]

U.G.: Sir, that is good for the schoolboy's logic. You know? We don't indulge in that, we are not philosophers. How to sharpen our intellect? We are not metaphysicians. We are simple ordinary people. You know? We want to find out about this thing for ourselves. Not depend on anybody. I have to learn if I want to teach psychology. I have to go and learn that every other week. You, in your turn, have to create psychologists and run the whole business. That is understood, but as a fact it doesn't in any way change your life. Be honest! Once in your life, once in your life. You don't want to be honest with me. Your belief in any of those things does not mean a damn thing to you! At all! You may read Vedanta morning till evening. Sit there and discuss everlastingly. You know? Analyze everything. Find the root meanings of those words. It doesn't mean anything. It is only sharpening your intellect and it is not helping you at all. It has turned you into a frightened chicken. You are a frightened man. At least this much you can do—to be honest with yourself. To be ruthless with everything you experience, what it is that is giving you all these experiences? You can find out for yourself. You don't need anybody's help. How are you creating all these things?

It has not happened to you. What does it matter if there is reincarnation or not? I make fun of these things. I grew up in the Theosophical Society, in those days of the Krishnamurti world teacher business. When people met…ha-ha, it's amazing when you first meet somebody you say, "I am UG. What is your name?" You know, introductions. They would greet each other with, "I was Queen Victoria in my past life, who were you?" That was the way people greeted. It's amazing. I told myself, they have taken up for themselves all the great personages in history of man. And they always talk like that. Amazing!

And once I asked: If Ashoka is reincarnated as Olcott, the president of the Theosophical Society, you call that evolution or involution? And Blavatsky has all those stories. If you are interested you can read those twelve previous lives of J. Krishnamurti. And why his face always matched those in his previous lives also is beyond me. I must always look exactly the way I am even in my previous lives. But one thing is amazing—what we believe. You need to believe. Belief is all that is there. You will replace one belief with another belief, one illusion with another illusion, but you don't want to be free from belief.

You are doing it every day—only memorizing these things you see. See and tell me! You are not seeing. Seeing is the ending. Look! You are not looking. How can you look? You tell me.

Q: You mean this instrument is not the...

U.G.: There is no other instrument.

Q: Do you think this instrument will ever touch the life which you are talking about?

U.G.: It is not possible. Even if it touches life you will not know anything about that life—now or even then. These questions wouldn't be there, to understand life, the meaning of life, the purpose of life, go and find that out. There is no meaning in our life. Otherwise we are picking up some meaning in life, purpose in life.

That 90-year-old man—he was with Krishnamurti for 61 years. Very close. Every day they went for walks, talking and talking. This year he wanted me to go in the car along the same road that he went on to sit and discuss. If after 85 years you do not know the meaning of life when the hell are you going to find out the meaning of life?

Q: Is there any meaning at all?

U.G.: If I say no how does it help you or interest you? Everybody else says there is a meaning. Do you see any meaning? That's all. Do you see any meaning in life? If this is all that is there, going to the office, seeing all the patients you have, day after day, day after day, making money. If that is all...the questions arise only because we don't want to come to terms that all that we have done, all that we have experienced, all that we have done in our life is coming to an end. Is that all? If that is all, this becomes more meaningful and purposeful. Not that you will go astray.

What I am saying is that if you are not caught up in the right and wrong, good and bad, you will not do anything wrong. I assure you, guarantee you., that you will not do anything wrong. If you do something wrong you pay the price for it. Whatever the society says you pay the price for it. Otherwise you can't do anything wrong. As long as we are moving between the two, the right and wrong, the good and bad, the good and evil, we will always do the evil things.

Q: Always do the evil things?

U.G.: Do something! There is a beautiful woman there. What will she do if I grabbed her? Grab and see what happens. She will slap you. That is the action. You are not doing anything. It has already done itself. That beauty has touched you but you are not acting. So going astray…go astray! So what happens?

Q: You get slapped, that's all.

U.G.: That's the action. Enjoy that. And maybe she will say "C'mon buddy."

What will happen there? I get slapped, take her out, and enjoy. Thank you!

Q: One last question.

U.G.: Yes, go ahead.

Q: This state which you have stumbled into, does it touch the totality of life?

U.G.: I don't know anything about it. Really! The question "to know" is not there. Not at all. You will never know that it is there. Now or even then. It is not my state.

Q: No, the state which you are in.

U.G.: This is the only state. I do not know any other state. Thank you. Anyway…he brought out all this…I'm not angry. Sometimes the energy….

What's that? Why are you amused? You don't tell me…you question that. Be honest with yourself. You have not many more years left.

Q: You say be honest with yourself. The next question I shall ask is: shall I find out who I am?

U.G.: What the hell? You think there is something here other than that question "Who am I?". That's all that is there. If there is nothing there to find the question cannot stay there. "Who am I here?" I repeat that question and that's the end of the question.

Q: Can I answer the question…

U.G.: Why are you waiting for an answer?!

Q: If I don't…

U.G.: No answer there! "Who am I?", first of all, is an idiotic question, born out of the assumption that there is something there, the nature of which you do not know, and the joker there threw that question at you, or "try this and find out". So the "Who am I?"… First of all, I have never asked that question. Even if I force myself to ask that question—who am I? Who. Am. I. Three words. That's all. There is no answer there. So the question cannot stay there. How can it stay there? Any answer you get for that question is what is put in there by others.

Q: So there's no way of finding myself?

U.G.: No, not at all.

Q: Even exploring the three states: dream, sleep and wakeful state?

U.G.: Are you awake?

Q: I will find out.

U.G.: Yes, find out.

[Laughter]

And you don't bother about sleep and dream. Now they say that with the dream you entertain yourself. The dreams are not necessary. It's a way of entertaining yourself. Do you know about sleep? I don't know a thing about sleep.

Q: In the sleep I don't know that I am sleeping.

U.G.: Yes. How do you know that you are awake?

Q: All my thought is...

U.G.: You are making statements—you are awake. Now are you awake? You assume that you are awake.

Q: When I wake up after I'm asleep...

U.G.: No, forget about the sleep. Now we deal with your wakeful state, huh? You are awake now. Are you? You are thinking!

Q: I think that I am awake. I find out.

U.G.: Don't bother about finding out! Don't bother about finding out.

Q: Even these discoveries which have been taking place all these years have come out of questioning only. If you don't question, you go back.

U.G.: Yeah, so what? What benefit has it to you? You have learned a lot about this body, and then you are helping me, correcting my sight, operating my cataracts. And why is it so important? The questions in that area are quite different from the questions you are asking about *Who am I?* That's all that I am asking.

Q: Maybe it's only questions and no answers.

U.G.: No, those answers have proofs in here. There is no proof there. That's all that I am saying. Why one day? I want that proof now. You are copping out. I want the answer now, about the I.

Q: Stop thinking about that.

U.G.: If you stop thinking the question goes. The thinking cannot give the answer. What is there is only thinking, and that thinking is because of a joker who threw that question at you—Who am I?—and he sings a song. "I am not this body, I am not causal body, I am not mental body." What the hell are you? He has a song. Who the hell are you?

"Who Am I?" Sing that song. C'mon, entertain us! Come, come! She will record it. "Who am I? Who am I?" Sing that song. Yes, sir. C'mon. We will end this with a song. Yes, go ahead. Entertain us. Yes. He will record it. It's more interesting than this talk. Yes, good. Don't go away sir!

[Singing]

Who am I? Who am I? Who am I?
Ramana guru says, Who am I?
Who am I? Who am I? Who am I?
Ramana guru says, Who am I?

God's body, not I.
Subtle body, not I.
Causal body, not I.

Then Who am I? Who am I? Who am I?
Ramana guru says, Who am I?

Sleeping state, not I.
Dreaming state, not I.
Waking state, not I.

Then Who am I? Who am I? Who am I?
Ramana guru says, Who am I?

Past time, not I.
Present time, not I.
Future time, not I.

Then Who am I? Who am I? Who am I?
Ramana guru says, Who am I?

After three states, and also three bodies.
After three states, and after three bodies.
After three times, and also the [inaudible].
I am the witness.

Chapter Six

WE ARE USING
A DEAD INSTRUMENT

Not in conflict with society. This is the only reality I have. The world as it is today. The ultimate reality that man has invented has absolutely no relationship whatsoever to the reality of this world. So as long as you are seeking searching , wanting to understand that reality which you call ultimate reality or call it by whatever name you like, so long it will not be possible for you to come to terms with the reality of the world exactly the way it is.

So anything you do to escape from the reality of this world will make it difficult for you to live in harmony with the things around you. So we have an idea of harmony. So how to live at peace with yourself? That's an idea. But already there is an extraordinary peace there. So what makes it difficult for you to live at peace with yourself is the creation of what you call peace which is totally unrelated to the harmonious functioning of this body.

When you free yourself from the burden of reaching out there to grasp, to experience, and to be in that reality, then you find it that it is more difficult to understand the reality of anything. You have no way of experiencing the reality of anything. So at least you are not living a world of illusions. You accept that there is nothing, nothing that you can do to experience the reality of anything. Except the reality that is imposed on us by the society. So we have to accept the reality as it is imposed on us by the society because it is very essential for us to function in this world intelligently and sanely. So if we don't accept that reality we are lost. So we end up in the loony bin. So we have to accept the reality as it is imposed on us by culture, by society or whatever you want to call it. And at the same time understand there's nothing that you can do to experience the reality of anything. Then you cannot be in conflict with society. And also the demand to be something other than what you are also comes to an end. It is the goal that you have placed before yourself. Rather, it is the goal that you have accepted as the ideal goal to be reached. The demand to be something other than what you are also is not there. It is not a question of accepting it. It is the pursuit of those goals which the culture has placed before us, the goals that we have accepted as the desirable ones, which is not there anymore. So, the demand to reach that goal is also not there anymore. You are what you are.

The movement in the direction of something other than what you are isn't there anymore. So you are not in conflict with yourself. If you are not in conflict with yourself you cannot be in conflict with the society around you. So if you are not at peace with yourself, it's not possible for you to be at peace with others. Even then, there is no guarantee that your neighbors will be peaceful. You see, you are not concerned with that. You are at peace with yourself, and the consequences of which are really difficult to face. Then you become a threat to this society, as it functions today. You become a threat to your neighbors also. Because they have accepted the reality of the world as real, and they are pursuing some funny thing called peace. So you will become a threat to their existence as they know it and as they experience it.

You are all alone. Not the aloneness that people want to avoid. You are all alone. It's not the intimate reality that one is interested in. All the techniques and systems and methods that he is using to achieve whatever the goal is, you know? The running of the motor there....not the teachings of the gurus, not the teachings of the holy men, not the techniques, umpteen number of them you have which will give you the energy which you are seeking. But that one, you see, that movement that is not there is the thing that will set in motion and release the energy that is there. It doesn't have to be any techniques that man has invented because there is no fiction there. You really don't know what it is. So the movement there and the movement here is one. There is energy there.

This is also [pointing to body] a mechanical energy. The human machine is no different from any machine out there. Both of them are in one unison. Whatever energy is there the same energy is in operation here. Any other energy you experience through the practice of any techniques is frictional energy. That energy is created by the friction of thought. The demand to experience that energy is the one that is responsible for the energy that you experience. But this energy is something which cannot be experienced at all. This is just an expression of the manifestation of life. You don't have to do a thing. Anything you do to experience that is preventing the possibility of that energy that is already there, which is the expression of life, manifestation of life, to function there.

But it has no value in terms of the values we give to whatever we are doing. The techniques, meditation, yoga and all that. I am not against any one of those things. Please don't get me wrong. But they are not the means to achieve the goal that you have placed before yourself. The goal itself is false. If the suppleness of the body is the goal you have before you, probably the techniques of yoga will certainly help to keep the body supple. That is not the instrument to reach the goal of enlightenment or transformation or whatever you want to call it. Or even the techniques of meditation. All those are the self-centered activities. They are all self-perpetuating mechanisms which you use. The object of your search for the ultimate reality is defeated by all these techniques because these techniques are self-perpetuating instruments which you are using.

And then you will certainly realize, or it dawns on you, that the very search for the ultimate reality is also a self-perpetuating mechanism. There is nothing to reach and nothing to gain, nothing to attain. So as long as you are doing something to attain whatever your goal is, this is a self-perpetuating mechanism. When I use the phrase "self-perpetuating mechanism" I don't mean that there is a self or an entity, but that it has this self-perpetuating mechanism. I have to use the word "self". There is no other word. The self starter you have in the car. You self-igniting things. Like that, you know? It perpetuates itself. That's all that it is interested in.

Anything you want to achieve is a self-centered activity. When I use the word self-centered activity, it is always translated in terms of something that has to be avoided. Because selflessness is the goal before you. As long as you are doing something to be selfless, you are a self-centered individual. So when this movement in the direction of wanting to be a selfless man is not there then there is no self, there is no self-centered activity.

The techniques which you are using, the systems and methods which you are using to reach your goal of selflessness is itself a self-centered activity. So when once that demand is not there anymore... But if the society or the culture or whatever you want to call it has placed before us a perfect goal, the ideal goal, that's the goal of everybody because a selfless man will be a great asset to the society.

And the society is interested only in continuity. The *status quo*. So all those values which we have accepted as values that one should cultivate are invented by the human mind to keep itself going. The goal is the one that is making it possible for you to continue this way. But you are not getting anywhere, you see? The hope that one day through some miracle or through the help of somebody you will be able to reach the goal... It is the hope that keeps you going. But actually and factually you are not getting anywhere. You will realize somewhere along the line that whatever you are doing to reach your goal is not leading you anywhere. But then you want to try this, that and the other, but if you try one, that's it. All the other systems are exactly the same.

But this has to be very, very clear. Whatever pursuit you are indulging in, if I may use that word, somewhere along the line it has to dawn on you that it is not leading you anywhere. So as long as you want something you will do that. You see? That want has to be very clear. What do you want? That is why all the time I am asking that question. What do you want? "I want to be at peace with myself." You see? So that is an impossible goal for you because everything you are doing to get peace with yourself is the one that is destroying the peace that is already there. You have set in motion, at the moment of thought, the destruction of the peace that is there. I don't know if it is clear to you or not.

It's very difficult to understand that. All that you are doing is the impediment, is the one that is disturbing the harmony and peace that is already there. Any movement in any direction on any level is a very destructive factor for the peaceful functioning of this living organism, which is not at all interested in your spiritual experiences. It has no interest in any one of those spiritual experiences, however extraordinary they may be. Once you have one spiritual experience there is bound to be a demand for more and more of the same, and ultimately you will want to be in a permanent state.

There is no such thing as permanent happiness, permanent bliss at all. You think there is because all those books talk of eternal bliss, permanent bliss, permanent happiness. You know very well that it is not leading you anywhere. The mechanism that is involved, the instrument that you are using, is the one that keeps you going because it does not know anything else, it has come into being through so many years of hard work, effort and will. That itself is effort, that itself is will. You wanting to be in state of effortlessness through the use of effort is not going to succeed. So forget about the effortless state. It doesn't exist at all. If you want to be in an effortless state through effort, how the hell are you going to achieve that goal? You forget that everything you are doing, every movement that is there, every w ant that is there for whatever reason you want to be in an effortless state, is effort! So you cannot achieve that goal of effortlessness. Effortlessness is something which cannot be achieve through effort.

Is there anything that you can do to stop the effort? Even that also is an effort. It's really a maddening thing. Thank God you have not really pushed yourself into that corner. Then you will really go crazy. You are frightened of that, you see? That is impossible. You have to see that everything you are doing to be in that effortless state for whatever reason you want to be in there is effort. Even wanting not to use effort also is effort. The total absence of will, and the total absence of effort of all kinds may be called an effortless state, but that effortless state is not something that you can achieve through effort.

I don't know if it is understood the meaninglessness of what you are doing. You can change the techniques, you can change the teachers, but basically and essentially, the very teaching that you are using to reach your goal is the obstacle. It doesn't matter what teacher you follow. If you question the teaching you have to question the teacher himself. So therein comes the sentiment. "Something is wrong with me." "One day I am going to understand."

So if it not possible for you to understand today, you are not going to understand at all. So the understanding is the absence of the demand for understanding. Either now or tomorrow, see? Now there is no understanding necessary. The understanding is only for the purpose of understanding something. Tomorrow, not today. Today you don't have to understand a thing at all. It may sound funny to you but that's the way it is.

So what do you want to understand? You can't understand me at all. I've been talking about it for 20 days. I can go on but you are not going to understand anything. It's not that it is difficult—it's so simple. The complex structure that is involved is the very thing that's not accepting the simplicity of it. That is really the problem. "It can't be that simple." Because that structure is so complex that it doesn't want even to consider the possibility that it could be so simple. So you are going to understand tomorrow, not today. Tomorrow is the same story, and then after 10 years, it's the same story. So what do you do about this situation? If you push yourself into the corner you are not going to do that anymore.

What do you want to understand? I'm not saying anything profound! I've been repeating the same thing day after day. It's not something that the thought is manufacturing here. It's not a thought manufactured or a logically certain premise that I'm putting across to you. Basically, it sounds very contradictory to you. What actually I am doing you don't understand. I make a statement, and the 2nd statement is negating the first statement. Sometimes you see some contradictions in what I am saying. Actually they are not contradictions. So this statement does not express what I am trying to express. The second statement is negating the first statement. And the third statement is negating the first two statements. The fourth statement is negating the previous three statements. Not with the idea of arriving at any goal. Not with the idea of communicating to you. There is nothing to be communicated. Only a series of negations—not with the idea of arriving at any goal.

The goal is understanding, you know? So you want to understand. There is nothing to understand here. Every time you make some sense out of it, I'm trying to point out that's not it. It is not the doctrine of neti-neti, it doesn't involve this negative approach. But the so-called negative approach is a positive approach. Because still they are interested in reaching the goal. So they have failed this through their positive approaches, they have invented what is called the "negative approach." Not this, not this, not this. The unknown cannot be reached, or cannot be experienced, with true positive approach. So they have failed. So then, you see, this so-called negative approach is not really a negative approach because the goal is still a positive goal of knowing the unknown, for example. Or wanting to experience something which cannot be experienced.

So this movement, which has adopted a negative approach, is still interested in the positive goal. Knowing the unknown, experiencing something which cannot be experienced. It's only a trick, that's all it is. Playing with itself. As long as the goal is the positive goal, no matter what the goal is, any approach, whether it is called positive or negative is not a negative approach—it's a positive approach.

There is no such thing as the beyond, no such thing as the unknown. If you accept that there is such a thing as the unknown you will do something or the other to know the unknown. Your interest is to know. So this movement is not going to stop as long as it is interested in experiencing something that cannot be experienced. That means that there is still something which cannot be experienced. So there is no such a thing as the unknown at all. So can you say there is no such thing as the unknown—how can you make such a dogmatic assertion? You will find out. As long as you are pursuing the unknown, this movement is in operation. There is something that you can do, so that gives you the hope. Maybe one day you will stumble into this, to experience the unknown.

How can it, if there is any unknown, ever become part of the known? Not a chance. Even assuming for a moment that this movement, which is demanding to know the unknown, is not there, what is there—you will never know. You have no way of knowing that at all, no way of capturing that and experiencing that, or giving expression to it. So you talk of that bliss, eternal bliss, love and all that sort of romantic poetry because you have no way of capturing that and containing it and giving expression to it. So this dawns on you that this is not the movement, this is not the instrument that can help you to understand anything, and there is no other instrument. So then there is nothing to understand.

If you translate what I am saying in terms of your values, in terms of ethical codes of conduct, you are really missing the point. It's not that I'm against moral codes of conduct. You see, they have a social value. You understand? For the smooth functioning of society they are essential. But you will have to have some sort of conduct for functioning in this world intelligently. Otherwise, there will be utter chaos in this world. That is essential. That's a social problem. It is not an ethical problem, it is not a religious problem at all. You have to separate the two things—we are living in a different world today.

Not because they are bad, but because they are unsuitable for the present occasion. We have to find out some other way of keeping ourselves in harmony with the world around us. But as long as you are in conflict with yourselves, it is not possible for you to be in harmony with this society around you. So you are yourself responsible for that. It is not the world that is a messy world, but…

Q: How can one be responsible?

U.G.: What exactly do you mean by responsible? What do you mean?

Q: I don't think it exists.

U.G.: What exactly do you mean by responsibility? If you are not talking of responsibility that doesn't mean that you are responsible. You can't be responsible at all. It is disturbing. If you are interested in the smooth running of society, you necessarily have to be responsible. I don't know exactly what you mean by responsible—to fit yourself into the framework of the society? There is what you call responsibility. So if you demand rights, you have duties. You can't have rights without duties.

Us, here in the West the demand for rights only. You ignore the duties that go with the demand for rights. In the other part of the world, especially India, you have no rights but only duties—that's equally bad. So we have to establish harmonious relationship between the understandable, meaningful relationship between your duties and rights. I don't have any rights in this world, so I don't have duties—except the duties that I have towards my fellow beings. I cannot destroy anything in this world. I cannot do anything. I just can't. It's impossible for me to. Not because I am a responsible man or anything. It cannot dispossess anybody of anything for any reason.

The Communist thinks that I am a Communist. I am not a Communist because I don't want to dispossess anybody of anything. You can have everything you want. And I'm the last person to dispossess you of anything, because you will be unhappy. Why should I cause you unhappiness? For the sake of treating the poor? They will become more unhappy then.

I don't know exactly what you mean by responsibility. Any harm you do to anybody is harming you. You know? If I hurt somebody it is hurting physically, not psychologically, or in a fantasy way. If I hurt somebody physically, it hurts me physically. So I can't do that, you see?—to anybody.

So psychologically you can do anything. "You should not hurt anybody." "You should not hurt the feelings of others", and all that kind of thing. "You should be sensitive to the people around you—to the world around you—sensitive to the plants, sensitive to everything"—you see? That's all just talking. It has to come down to the level of physical hurt. If you hurt somebody it's going to hurt you also. Then you can't hurt anybody. So I don't go around calling myself a responsible man.

If you cut the hand of somebody, is it going to hurt you? Yes, it's going to hurt you. Your finger may not come off, but the physical pain is shared there, you see? It's not a shared feeling—it's the same. The pain is exactly the same. You may not bleed there, but still it is a very painful thing for you all. You cannot harm anybody for any reason. It has to be brought down to the level of physical hurt, otherwise you will manipulate things, manage things.

As long as the policemen was there inside of you, which religion very successfully managed to do—fear of hell, fear of this, fear of that, you see? You know, things were running smoothly. Now it's very easy to cheat a policeman *out* there. You can manipulate. You can bribe him. Do anything you want. Both are there now: the inside policeman as well as the policeman *out there*. You have lost faith in both. In that we need him to protect our kids. Do you not want a policemen to protect your things? That's for you to decide. Your life, your property, everything.

If you translate these statements that I'm making and put them in the framework of your religious thinking you are really missing the point. It has nothing to with it at all. I'm not suggesting that you should change yourself into something other than what you are. It is just not possible. I am not trying to free you from anything. I don't think there is any purpose in this talking. But in the light of the description maybe you will realize that the image you have of whatever you are after has no relationship whatsoever. So you can brush aside my description and say it is nonsense. That's your privilege. Maybe it will occur to you that the image you have of your goal, or the image you have of what you are going to be one day, through all the effort and will that you are using, has absolutely no relationship whatsoever with what I am describing. This is not really what you are interested in. You know?

I was telling you the other day: I wish I could give you just a glimpse of it. Not glimpse in the sense that you use the world glimpse…a touch of it. You wouldn't want to touch this at all. And what you want, what you are interested in, doesn't exist. You can have a lot of petty experiences. If that is what you are interested in do all the meditations. Do everything you want. You'll have lots of them. It's a lot easier to experience those things by taking drugs. I'm not recommending drugs. They are the same. You know? Exactly the same. And the doctors say that that will damage the brain. Some of those things will also damage the brain if it is done very seriously. That's why they have all gone crazy—jumped into the river and killed themselves. They did all kinds of things. They locked themselves up in caves because they couldn't face it. You know?

It's not possible for you to watch your thoughts, not possible for you to watch every step you take. You see? You can't walk. That's not what is meant by the idea that you should be aware of everything. How is it possible for you to watch everything? Every thought of yours? And why do you want to watch your thoughts? What for? Control? It's not possible for you to control. It is a tremendous momentum.

When you imagine that you have controlled your thoughts and experience some space between two thoughts or some thoughtless state, you feel that you are getting somewhere. That is a thought-induced state of thoughtlessness. That's a thought-induced space between two thoughts. The fact that you experience those states, space between two thoughts, and thoughtless state, means that the thought was very much there. You know? So it surfaces afterwards. Like the river that flows through France—somewhere it disappears, then comes up again. It has gone underground. It does not mean that the river is not there. It is still there. You cannot use it for the purposes of navigation. But ultimately it comes up again and reaches the ocean in exactly the same way that you are pushing it down to the subterranean regions and feel that you are experiencing something extraordinary, but it surfaces. Then you find that the thoughts are welling up inside of you. You are not aware that you breathing now. You don't have to be conscious of your breathing. Why do you want to be conscious of your breathing? To control your breathing? Expand your lungs, do what you like. That's a different matter.

Why do you want to be aware of the movement of breath from the origin to the end? Then you suddenly become conscious of your breathing. Your breath and thought are very closely related. That's why you want to control your breath. And that, in a way, is controlling thought for awhile. But if you hold your breath for too long, it's going to choke you to death. In exactly the same way, anything you do to hold it, block the flow of thoughts, is going to choke you to death, literally to death. Or it will damage something there. It is a very powerful vibration.

What is thought? Thought is, after all, a vibration. Extraordinary vibration. It is like an atom. You can't play with those things at all. Except the petty experiences you have when you manipulate those things. For what purpose? You are not going to reach your goal of completely controlling your thought. It has to function in its own way—in its disconnected, disjointed way. That is something which cannot be brought about through any effort of yours. It has to fall to its normal rhythm. So even if you want to make it fall into the normal rhythm, you are adding momentum to that. That has a life of its own. It has, unfortunately, established a parallel life—the movement of life. These two are always in conflict. That will come to an end only when that body becomes deceased.

As I was saying yesterday the thought has become the master of this body. It's not totally mastered the whole thing. It's still trying to control everything that is there. You cannot pull the servant out of the household no matter what you do. If you forcibly do it he will burn the whole household, knowing very well that he will also be burned—it's a foolish thing for him but that's what he's going to do. But don't push these similes to the logical conclusions. Find out for yourself when you do these things...not just take them lightly. Take them lightly and play with them—that's all.

Q: So, just float?

U.G.: Floating is not a voluntary thing on your part. You don't have to do a thing. You are not separate from that. That's all that I am emphasizing. You cannot separate yourself from the thought and say these are my thoughts. That is the illusion you have. You cannot be without any illusion. You always replace one illusion with another illusion. Always!

Q: And I accept that as well in myself?

U.G.: You accept that you are always replacing one illusion with another illusion. So you wanting to be free from illusion is an impossibility. That itself is an illusion. So why do you want to be free from illusions? That's the end of you! It's not that I'm frightening you. I'm just pointing out that it is not just a light-hearted game to play. That is you. You as you know yourself. That knowledge you have of yourself is not there anymore. You can't be there anymore. So when it is not there the knowledge you have of the world also is not there anymore. It can't be there anymore. It is not going to come to an end. That is the end, you see? It will always be replaced by another illusion.

So you don't want to be a normal person, you don't want to be an ordinary person. That is really the problem. It's the most difficult thing is to be an ordinary person. Culture demands that you must be something other than what you are. That has set in momentum this tremendous, powerful movement of thought which demands that you should be something other than what you are. That's all that is there. You use it to achieve something. I don't know if it has no use. The only use you have for the thought is to feed this body. Without thought you cannot, you won't. That is why thought is there, and to reproduce one like this. That's all the use you have for the thought. It has no other use at all. It cannot be used to speculate, you see?

You can have a tremendous philosophical structure of thought but it has no value at all. You can interpret it, you see? Any event in your life. The events around you build up another philosophical structure of thought. That's not intended for that. But at the same time you forget that everything you have around you is the creation of thought. You are yourself born out of this thought. Otherwise you wouldn't be here at all. In that sense it has a tremendous value. Yet, that is the very thing that will destroy you. That's the paradox. Everything that you have created in this world has become possible through the help of that thought, but that very thing has become the enemy of man. You are using that for purposes which it is not interested in: solving the living problems. It can be used for solving the technical problems very well and efficiently, but it is not something which cannot be used to solve the problems of life.

Positive thinking, positive living...very interesting. You can't be always positive. How can you be always positive? So anything that is not suggesting your positive thing you call it negative. The positive and negative is only in the field of your thinking. When the thought is not there it is neither positive nor negative. As I was saying there is no such thing as a negative approach at all. It's a gimmick to play with.

Stand on your own feet. You can walk. You can swim. You are not going to sink. That's all that I can say. As long as there is a fear, the danger of your thinking there is almost certain. Otherwise there is buoyancy there in the water that keeps you afloat. Your fear of sinking is the very thing that makes it impossible for you to let the movement move in its own way. You see? It has no direction. It's just a movement. It has no direction. You are all the time trying to manipulate, trying to channel that particular direction so that you can have some benefits out of it. It is just a movement without a direction.

I can repeat the same thing in different words. That's what I have been doing all the time. If you read this you will be surprised how repetitive the whole thing is.

Q: Why this rather funny animal is thinking all the time? Why? And just building all those thoughts? Not just...

U.G.: you tell me. When do you think? Not *why* do you think. *When* do you think? I'm asking you a question. When do you think?

Q: As far as I know all the time.

U.G.: All the time. What is responsible for your thinking? You haven't yet answered my question. When do you think? When you want something, you think. It's very clear to me.

Q: Not at all.

U.G.: You don't even know that you are thinking, you see? Do you know that you are thinking now? It's an automatic thing.

Q: It's an automatic thing.

U.G.: You don't even know that you are thinking. So why this sudden interest in finding out why you are thinking? I don't even know that I'm talking. You don't even know that you are talking. You know? When you ask your question, am I thinking? You say yes. You would say yes. That yes is also an automatic thing.

Q: I don't care if it's automatic or not, a lot of automatic things...

U.G.: The whole thing is an automatic one. Whatever is put in there, when you are stimulated, it comes out. You see? To use the jargon of a computer language the input has to be there. You understand? So this has been going on and on and on and on. When there is stimulation, it comes out. That's the reason why you go on acquiring this knowledge, feeding it all the time. It's a computer. After all, it's an automatic thing that is there.

What do you know? You know a lot. You have gathered all this from various sources, filling it up. Most of it is not necessary. So you *know* a lot, and you want to know more and more and more and more. To use it, you see? Of course. There is no such thing as knowledge for the sake of knowledge. It used to be a power. Knowledge is power. You see?

"I know—you don't know." That gives you power. You may not even be conscious of that, you see? You knowing more than the other gives you a power. In that sense knowledge is power. And to acquire more and more knowledge other than the knowledge that is essential for the survival of the living organism is to acquire more and more power over others.

Except the technical knowledge that you need to make a living. That is understandable. That's all. I have to learn a technique. The society is not going to feed me unless I give something in return. You have to give what they want, not what you have to give. Otherwise, what value has this knowledge for you? All the time we are talking about thought and thinking and if somebody asks you question, which I am doing, what is thought?

Have you ever looked at thought? Let alone controlling thought, let alone manipulating thought, let alone using that thought for achieving something, material or otherwise. You cannot look at your thought because you cannot separate yourself from thought and look at it. The illusion that you have is the knowledge you have about thought. That is all that is there. There is no thought independent or apart from the knowledge or definitions you have about those thoughts.

So if someone asks the question—what is thought?—any answer you have is the answer that is put in there, the answers that others have given. And by combinations and permutations of those ideations and mentations about thoughts, you have created your own thoughts, which you call your own. Just like mixing up different colors you create, I don't know, thousands of pastel colors we have. Basically all of them can be reduced to only several colors that you find in nature. So even the seven colors you see, they are not actually seven. I don't want to go into that whole philosophy and nature and all that.

What you think is yours is actually the combination and permutation of all those thoughts—just the way that you have created hundreds and hundreds of pastel colors. You have created your own ideas—that is what you call thinking. But when you want to look at thought, what is there is only what you know about thought. Otherwise you can't look at thought.

There is no thought other than what is there, what you know about thought. This is what I'm saying. When that is understood, the meaninglessness of the whole business of wanting to look at thought comes to an end. Because it's not possible. What is there is only what you know, the definitions given by others. And out of those definitions, if you are very intelligent and clever enough, you create your own definitions. That's all.

So it is like any other *object* you have around you. There are so many objects, you know? When you look at it the knowledge you have about that comes into your head. There is an illusion that the thought is something different. It is you that create the object. The object may be there but the knowledge you have about that object is all that you know apart from that knowledge. Independent of that knowledge, free from that knowledge, you have no way of knowing anything about it.

You have no way of directly experiencing anything. We started with that. When I use the word directly it does not mean that there is any other way of experiencing things. That is the wrong word: directly. It implies that there is some other way of experiencing things directly other than the way you are experiencing things. The knowledge you have about it is all that is there and is what you are experiencing. Really, you don't know what it is.

In exactly the same way, when you want to know something about thought, experience thought, it is the same process that is in operation there. There is no inside and outside. What is there is only the operation, the flow of the knowledge. You cannot actually separate yourself from thought and look at it.

When once such a question is thrown at you what should happen is that the answers lose their meaning, because all that is acquired in thought. So that movement stops. There is no need for you to answer the question. There is no need for you to know anything about it. All that you know comes to a halt. Not literally. It simply has no momentum anymore. It slows down.

Then it dawns upon you the meaninglessness of trying to answer that question, because it really has no answer at all. The answers that others have given are there. So you have nothing to say on that thing called thought because all that you can say is what you have gathered from others, so you have no answer of your own.

Q: Apart from the question whether it is meaningful or meaningless there is something here—walls and things and people, and what we know about this, what we see about it, that's what we...

U.G.: But that is not what that person is. You don't know actually anything about that person or that thing. Except what you are projecting on that object or the individual—the knowledge you have about it. And this knowledge is experience. It goes on and on—that's all. What that really are you have no way of knowing it.

Q: That is what I do understand. When we are speaking about real things we can speak of knowledge about it, and call this knowledge reality, and we can speak about that which the knowledge is applied to.

U.G.: What for? Then it becomes a classroom discussion or the discussion of a debating society. Each one trying to show that he knows more, a lot more than the other. And arriving at what? What do you get out of it? Each one is trying to prove that he knows more than you do, to bring you over to his point of view.

Q: What I am trying to ask is: is there any chance of getting out of this knowledge of reality to reality itself?

U.G.: If you are lucky enough—it's only luck—to get out of this trap of knowledge, the question of reality is not there anymore. Because the question is thrown out by this knowledge, which is still interested in finding out the reality of things—and to experience for yourself directly what the reality is all about. So when this is not there the question is also not there. There is no need for finding out any answer. Because this question which you are posing to yourself, and also putting to me, is born out of the assumption that there is reality, and the assumption is born out of this knowledge you have of and about the reality.

When this is not there the knowledge is not there...the knowledge is the answer you already have. That is why you are asking the question. The question automatically goes. What is necessary is not to find out the answer for the question but understand that the question which you are asking, posing to yourself and putting to somebody else, is born out of the answer you already have, which is the knowledge. The question and answer format becomes a meaningless ritual.

But if you are really interested in finding out the reality it has to dawn on you that your very questioning mechanism is born out of the answers that you already have. Otherwise there can't be any questions.

First of all, there is an assumption on your part that there is reality. And then that there is something that you can do to experience the reality of things, without the knowledge. Knowledge gives you the experience of reality. That is for sure. If this is not there, is there any other of experiencing the reality? You are asking the question. The question goes with the answer. So there is no need to ask questions and there is no need to answer.

I'm not trying to be clever. I'm just trying to spotlight what is involved in the question and answer business. I'm not actually answering any of your questions. I'm just pointing out you cannot have any questions. What you have are the answers.

Q: I do understand. Even then I would like to continue the game.

U.G.: Fine. Maybe you are good at the game. I am not. Anyway, we'll see what we can do.

Q: Even though you know our preoccupation with knowledge about thought, about anything, you are talking about reality to us, and about accepting reality...

U.G.: As it is.

Q: As it is...

U.G.: As it is imposed on us by our culture for purposes of intelligent and sane functioning in this world. And yet realizing that it has no other value other than the functional value. Otherwise we will be in trouble, you see? If you don't call this a "microphone" but instead decide to call it a monkey tomorrow, we would all re-learn, and every time we look at it call it a red or black monkey instead of a microphone. That's all, you see? It's very simple. It's for purposes of communication.

Q: I wonder what would happen if you do.

U.G.: What?

Q: Call that a monkey and a this or a that, because a lot of philosophies and ideas are also linked to that.

U.G.: No, it's interesting to build a philosophical structure. That's why we have so many philosophers, so many philosophies in this world.

Q: There's only one possibility to strive after accepting, for every strive without accepting is not...

U.G.: don't you see the contradiction in those terms? If you accept, where is the need for striving?

Q: I'm not sure.

U.G.: It comes to an end. If you accept something you cannot talk of striving there at all. You're accepting. You believe. You believe in something. You accept it as an act of faith, and that's the end of it. So, you can't say it as a question. That means you have not accepted it. You are not sure of it.

Q: I have to accept my job as a legal officer before I could strive to...

U.G.: So, you see, you had to struggle, put a lot of effort to acquire the necessary legal knowledge to get this job. That is understood, you see? So that is the only way. There is no other way. And you are applying that technique to achieve the so-called spiritual goals. This is the difference that I am pointing out.

What do they do in the courts? You have always to rely upon the precedents, the previous judgments. Both lawyers call to previous judgments and argue it out, and the judge either accepts yours or the other fellow's, and gives the decision either in favor of your client or the other client. Alright.

So then there is a higher court. You go to a higher court. They are the same. And you go to the Supreme Court—there the judge finally decides: this is it. You can disagree with the judgment. The client can do everything possible to reject it and refuse to accept, but he has a way of enforcing that judgment through force. If it is a civil case, a civil suit, you will lose what you are claiming for. If there is a criminal thing you will end up in prison.

So ultimately that's the man who decides who is telling the lie and who is telling the truth. It is arbitrary. It is very essential for you to be conversant with the whole structure of law. I'm just pointing out that it is very essential to *know* the legal side of it and acquire the legal knowledge. It will get you your job. The more efficient you are the better are your chances; the cleverer you are the better are your prospects. That is understood.

So you have to put struggle and use effort, use your will, and then you have arrived at that point. There is always more and more to it. But all that is instrument which you are using to achieve your spiritual goals. That is all that I am pointing out.

That cannot conceive of the possibility of understanding anything except in time. It takes time. It has taken so many years for you to be where you are today. And you are still striving and struggling to reach a higher plateau, and higher and higher and higher. The hierarchy is there. So that instrument which you are using cannot conceive of the possibility of understanding anything without effort, without striving. It cannot conceive of this possibility.

But the issues that you have to deal with in life, the "living" issues—that is where this has not helped to solve the problems. Temporarily, you can find some solution, but that creates another problem, another problem and another problem—it goes on and on and on and on.

So that is something which cannot be used to tackle the live issues. These are all live issues. The living problems demand the instrument which is not dead. The instrument which we are using in other areas is a dead instrument, so that cannot be used to understand anything living. That is all that I am saying. You cannot but think in terms of striving, effort and time—that "one day you are going to reach the spiritual goal." It's like the way you have succeeded, or are still trying to succeed, at the goal which you have placed before you.

Q: But are you trying to say that there is some knowledge that shows the real problem of life?

U.G.: No, not at all. That cannot help you to understand or solve the living problems. Because, in that sense, there are no problems there at all. We only have the solutions. You are interested only in solutions, and those solutions have not solved your problems; so you are trying to find different kind of solutions, but the situation will remain exactly the same.

However, there is somehow the hope that you will find *the* solution for solving your problems. So your problem is not the problem, but the solution. See? When the solution is gone there is no problem there. You are not ready to accept that that is not the solution. If there is a solution the problem shouldn't be there anymore.

This is what I have to say. The answers are given by others, by wise men. The questions shouldn't be there at all. They are obviously not the answers. If they were the answers the questions wouldn't be there. So why don't you question the answers. If you question the answers you question those who have given the answers.

You take it for granted that they're all wise men, they're all spiritually superior to us all, and that they know what they are talking about. They don't what they are talking about. They don't know a damn thing. We stop now.

Chapter Seven

THE WORLD IS JUST AN IDEA

Q: Mr. U.G. Krishnamurti, since you don't believe in traditions, you don't believe in mind, and you don't believe in the existence of soul or any so-called internal human being, let me start with the first question. Why do you follow the tradition of keeping a name? Why do you carry a name? Why do you identify yourself as U.G. Krishnamurti? Because this is also part of a tradition.

U.G.: Yes, that this true. But you could give me a prisoner number. And many of the people who think they are enlightened people and those who give up, become Sannyasins, they have a new name. What actually happens when you don't use the name that is given to us to by our parents, it that you have to develop a new kind of identity there. So what is important to us is to maintain the identity.

When people ask me the question "What's your name?" it takes a little time for the computer to come up with the name U.G. Krishnamurti. Since Krishnamurti is such a common name and there were so many Krishnamurti's living at the time when I lived in Adyar, we all decided to use the initials U.G. So that is why everybody calls me U.G. My children call me U.G.

Q: But you see, naming is a part of a very complicated tradition. Krishnamurti itself, you know, denotes many things. It denotes Krishna, it denotes its incarnation, it denotes so many things. Why do you keep that name? Why haven't you changed it?

U.G.: As I said a while ago it doesn't make any difference whether I call myself Krishnamurti or use a number. Now it's a lot easier for these computers to handle numbers than with names. So you have a bank account with a number, home address with a number, a telephone number. It's a lot easier for the computer here to deal with the numbers than with the names given to us.

And to me the tradition is nothing but unwillingness on our part to change with the changing things. Things are changing constantly, and we are not ready to change and move along with the change in the things in our life. So we call it tradition and cover it up to feel that we are all very traditional people. Then the story begins. You have to create an identity there again with the number instrument. So it doesn't really matter whether I call myself Krishnamurti, 48592 or any other number.

Q: Fine. It seems you do not believe in philosophy, or you do not agree with the meaning of the world philosophy. And you say that you do not have anything to give, anything to convey. In that sense what should others call you? A philosopher? A revolutionary? A thinker or what? What would you like yourself to be termed as?

U.G.: No, I have the same problem. They asked me the question "Who the hell are you?" So to satisfy them I tell them that I'm a philosopher of some sort. You know the meaning of the word philosopher is a lover of wisdom.

I'm the luckiest man that has found that the totality of wisdom has a stranglehold on the people, and we are brainwashed to believe there is something extraordinary about the totality of wisdom that is passed down to us from generation to generation. We have been brainwashed for centuries to hold on to the great wisdom traditions that have been passed on to us from generation to generation. Because if you change your diet you think you will die. That's one of the reasons why we given tremendous importance to wisdom. As far as I'm concerned it doesn't mean a thing to me.

So people ask me "Who the hell are you?" I say that I am a philosopher of some sort. And I always have this problem when I go on radio programs like this or on television. They ask me the questions "Who are you?" or "Why the hell are you here?" "You have nothing to offer the individuals or the world at large."

My interest is to put across something which has happened to me, something extraordinary, and I know well that this is something which cannot be shared with others because it is not something...

Q: When did this happen?

U.G.: I do not know. I wish I knew. But something hit me.

Q: Why did it happen?

U.G.: Because all my life I wanted to discover the self, find out the self, and the demand to bring about a change in me obsessed me for my formative years, and later on this question haunted me.

Q: But self sounds something like a soul. You're talking about something eternal, aren't you?

U.G.: No, nothing. You know the meaning of the word self is spirit. It's a Latin word. I don't want to deal with the etymological meaning of the word.

Q: Spiritual doesn't mean the body.

U.G.: There is nothing there other than this physical organism functioning with an extraordinary intelligence of its own. So if anybody who is interested in finding out if there is any spirit, if there is any soul, if there is a mind, if there is a psyche. It doesn't matter what name you use or if there is an identity there, if there is an "I" there.

How do we go about it? The only way to go about it is you have to free yourself from everything everybody has said about this before. What you see there is created by you. So the demand to fit ourselves in a value system created by our culture is the one that is sapping out a tremendous amount of energy. And so we are not able to deal with the living problems. The demand to fit ourselves into the value system is the cause of man's tragedy. And there is no point in replacing one value system with another value system. That is what you call revolution. That is what you call by fancy names. But revolution, to put it in my own favorite way, is to replace one value system with another value system. And so the question...

Q: But value is a very subjective term. Whatever you are saying can be termed as a value system itself.

U.G.: I don't think they can make anything out of this and turn this into a model. That is why I am asking people, for goodness sake, don't turn me into a model.

Q: Can I term you as a follower or as a proponent of Charva philosophy or Larva philosophy. It's a very old philosophical system that used to be in India.

U.G.: That is not an appropriate way of caging me into...I don't recommend that kind of a thing to the people. Because everything we are doing is a pleasure movement. Even the beauty you are interested in, the music you are interested in, is nothing but a pleasure movement. So I'm not against a pleasure movement at all. I'm not against anybody saying anything.

What I'm interested in doing is, to use my favorite phrases, to spotlight it and focus it, for them to get the hang of what I am trying to say. What I am trying to say is a very simple thing. There is no way you can figure it out. It's not that I'm trying to mystify this and make it difficult for people to get the hang of what I am trying to say.

I want to leave those listeners, the viewers, and those who come to see me, with this impossibility of figuring out what I am trying to put across. And so in that situation something extraordinary can happen to the individual. You'd be surprised to find out that once this stranglehold of everything that is taught to us, everything that we felt, everything that we experienced before, cannot manipulate these bodies, cannot force the actions to fit into a particular pattern or particular value system.

The whole value system is born out of the assumption that we have great spiritual teachers, and we have turned them into models. So the whole energy is consumed by that demand and our effort to fit ourselves to become copies of those models. So we don't have the guts, we don't have the courage to brush them aside.

There is no way you can brush them aside, no way you can free yourself from belief without replacing that belief with another belief. So belief is not actually a thing that is there. What is there is only a believer. And the believer thinks that he believes in something, so he separates the two. That is a very comforting thing for one who says that I believe in this or that.

So the belief is the most important thing. If the belief comes to an end the you as you know yourself, and the you as you experience yourself, also comes to an end. What you will be left with is anybody's guess. And you have no way of finding out what you are left with. But you just leave that alone to function with an extraordinary intelligent, alertness, alacrity. You are not any more interested in forcing yourself to be put into a value system. At the same time you do not become a rebel. You are not even a rebel without a cause, you are not a revolutionary—you are not any of those things. You are not in conflict with the society you are functioning in. Then it is possible for us to function sanely and intelligently.

Q: This sort-of anarchic description you have just given—do you call it enlightenment. Would you like to term it as enlightenment?

U.G.: I wouldn't use any of those names to describe...

Q: Is it a vacuum? What is it?

U.G.: If you say it's a vacuum it ceases to be a vacuum. If I may define it in my own particular and peculiar way, I would say it is a state of being and not a state of doing. An anarchist, if there is one in this world, would never destroy anything because if he tries to destroy the world around him he's also destroying himself. So anarchy is not the right word to use. But I maintain that if there is a state of anarchy, it is a state of being and not a state of doing. No action is born out of this state of anarchy. You will never be an anarchist to destroy anything because he cannot separate himself from the world around him.

Q: Do you believe in some sort of morality? Is there any place of morality in your system of thinking?

U.G.: When once you are not caught up within the right and wrong, good and bad, moral and immoral...

Q: How do you define good and bad, moral and immoral?

U.G.: They are all definitions given to us by our culture, you see? So we are all the time...

Q: And you would disregard culture. Would you re-define it then?

U.G.: What is the point in redefining it if you become another culture, and the whole cultural story will start all over again? You know, as a matter of fact, somebody asked me a question in one of those television interviews in India: "How do you want us to remember you 500 years after you're gone?" Why the hell do you want to remember me 500 years after I am dead and gone?

Q: That's a very large scale. What I am worried about is how a son, a mother, a father, a brother should behave towards each other. Do you believe in some sort of social morality or not?

U.G.: No, it's not question of belief. It doesn't operate in the lives of the people. We just talk about all those things. That's all. It doesn't operate in the lives of those people.

Q: No, if you are asking people to give away their cultural beliefs altogether...

U.G.: I am not asking them to give up their cultural beliefs. I'm not asking them to do anything. I want you to understand that what you believe in is not operating in your life. I found this in my own way—that the spiritual teachers and their lives would never be put together. There was a tremendous dichotomy, if I may use that nice-sounding word...

Q: Hypocrisy.

U.G.: I didn't want to use the word hypocrisy. Why is there this dichotomy in the lives of people? What they are saying is one thing, what they are doing is totally unrelated to what they are claiming to be. So there must be something wrong. This was my only obsession.

Q: No, but that is a reflection of our capacity because we always try to become ideals. We always try to follow the ideals but we cannot because we have human limitations.

U.G.: That is true. That is the hope we have, the hope that is created by our culture, that one day you are going to be a wonderful person. So when? So you are going to be free from all this 10 years from now, 20 years, and there comes a time when you die, if I may use that word. You invent a thing called reincarnation, and life after death goes on and on and on. Until then I remain what I am.

Q: No, but without hope one ceases to live anyway. I mean life becomes absolutely endless.

U.G.: Not at all. Without hope it is something extraordinary. The nature of that life is something which cannot be imagined.

Q: Do you in any case believe the karma theory, cause and effect, the principle of causality?

U.G.: You see, the word karma in Sanskrit means action. Any action that is born out of thought is destructive. Is there any action called a spontaneous action, pure action, outside the field of cause-and-effect? This is something which you will never know. Because the thought is operating in the field of cause and effect, and it has invented that cause is the effect and effect is the cause; and all that philosophical, metaphysical discussions that go on day after day, day after day. It's very interesting to listen to, but the cause and effect relationship is what you are all the time trying to relate and establish a relationship between.

But every event in life is an independent event. So you have to link up those two and create a story. This is "me". The only way you can create the story of your own life for yourself and others is to relate the two and tell how you can link up cause and effect relationship and tell a story about yourself and others.

Q: It is a basic physical principle. Every action creates a reaction.

U.G.: Not at all. Every event is an independent event. And we think that there cannot be any action...

Q: There is no correlation between two events?

U.G.: No, each event is an independent event.

Q: That means it's a Buddhist philosophy.

U.G.: I don't know what it is. Then if there is no relationship between the two you think that it's going to be a very chaotic way of living. I assure you that it is not going to be a chaotic way of living.

Q: Buddhist philosophy says: every moment ceases to be in itself.

U.G.: They have created a tremendous metaphysics, don't forget that.

Q: That was in reaction to Indian metaphysics.

U.G.: Whatever it is you cannot say there is a void there, that there is a *sunyata* there. So that is the reason why I don't accept the negative approach also. The negative approach is adopted by us because the positive approach to reach our goals has failed, and so we have invented a thing called a negative approach. But the negative approach is still related to the goal. Whatever is the goal—to be in a state of sunyata, to be an enlightened man, to be this or that, to be happy all the time.

So what anybody and everybody is interested in is one basic thing: how to be happy without one moment of unhappiness. I always repeat *ad nauseam*, if I may use that high-sounding phrase, to have pleasure without pain. So every sensation has a limited life. A span of life, you see? The demand to keep that particular sensation, which you call happiness, to last longer than its natural duration of life is the one that is causing all the unhappiness and pain.

This physical body is interested in maintaining its sensitivity. The more you try to keep the sensation of pleasure or the sensation of happiness to last longer you become an unhappy individual. So all those people are telling you: "I have a way to make you feel happy forever. To have pleasure without pain."

There is no way you can be happy without one moment of unhappiness. I tell people that I really do not know what happiness is in life, so I can never, never be unhappy. People ask me "Are you bored?" At no time I feel that there is something more interesting, more purposeful, more meaningful to do than what I am actually doing. So there is no such thing as boredom at all.

I am now talking and my interest is to see that I am in no way trying to influence you or trying to change your point of view or the point of the view of the people out there who are listening or not listening. So just to say things exactly the way they are, not the way I feel, not the way I think they should be. There is no point of view here.

You know the conversation between two persons is always to influence you, to change your point of view. I am not interested in changing your point of view, and there is no way you can change my point of view. So, in most cases, the dialogues and the conversations become meaningless to me, and ultimately in the final analysis, if I may say it so, it is a monologue.

Q: No, but it seems you are challenging the whole linguistic behavior in self, if I may say so. If you talk about the modern concept of linguistic philosophy, whatever you are saying, whatever phrases you are using, have a very strong cultural and social connotation. Would you like to challenge that?

U.G.: I am using that language to find out the absurdity of the individual to use language, to use logic, rationality and the knowledge he has to feel superior; to feel that he is a logical man, that he is a rational man and that he knows a lot more than I do. So that gives the feeling of goodness—that you know more than I do.

When I was a student in university, they were considered to be great professors. I used to tell myself: that fellow has read ten books; I have read only one book. So he's not honest enough, decent enough to admit to the students the source of his information. So why the hell do I have to listen to him?

I would walk out of the class; if I am interested in studying something I can get the same information from the books that he's reading. So he has read 20 books and I have read only one. He's a brilliant orator because he has practiced this art of elocution all his life; he is considered to be one of the greatest orators of our times. So how do I become the orator? Why I want to be an orator is altogether a different story. So that was all that I was interested in. What is it that he has that I don't have?

Whatever I see here is the opposite of what I wanted to be. So this is me. And why am I not enlightened? Because you should be enlightened; you are not happy because you should be happy. And what gives me happiness? If I get what I want I feel happy. If I don't get what I want I'm unhappy. So is there any such a thing as happiness at all? If you can get whatever you want then the question of unhappiness is not of relevance. But we have not succeeded in having one without the other: to be happy always without a moment of unhappiness.

So it is not a question of settling for or accepting the fact of the reality that you cannot always be happy, and that you have to settle for and accept the reality that you can be happy for some time and unhappy some other time.

Q: One basic purpose of ethics and morality is how to deal with others. How would you define that purpose?

U.G.: I will not do anything that will harm others because I am not separate from others.

Q: You believe in the old Indian ethical saying: [foreign language]?

U.G.: No, no. I don't even know what it means. Hurting my fellow being...

Q: It means don't do those things to others which you do not like to be done to you.

U.G.: Not at all. It is not that. It physically hurts me. I am never, never impressed by or affected by the psychological problems of the people. And once you are freed from the psychological info, you realize that what this *is* affected by is what is happening around you—the physical thing that is happening around you. If there is something that I can do to that individual who is suffering I will do it.

Q: Whatever you are saying so far can be interpreted in terms of basic biological or scientific facts. Scientists who deal in biology or scientists who deal in physical science can say all these things. What special you are conveying or saying? And what you would like to term yourself as?

U.G.: Well, some of those scientists come to see me for their own reasons. They tell me what I am saying is true, but they want to believe that I am wrong. The other thing is, they are all theorists. The scientist is just a metaphysician discussing everlastingly the things which do not operate in their lives.

Q: No, for example, you are talking about sensual stimulus which is a physical trait.

U.G.: But it is not translated into sensual activity at all. Because there is no space between the stimulus and the response. They can take me to a laboratory and do some experiments and hit me here and say this is the response to the stimulus. But actually and factually there is no way you can separate the two things. I do not use some metaphysical knowledge or religious stuff that is passed down to me. Actually and factually there is no space between the stimulus and response.

Q: That means you are saying something more than biological facts.

U.G.: I don't know. I don't claim. This is what I have found. This body is functioning with an extraordinary intelligence of its own, and whether it fits into their theories or not is not my interest. They can reject the whole thing and say its absolute rubbish.

Q: Does the world end with our body?

U.G.: The world doesn't exist for you even now. It is just an idea. What you are trying to experience, the world you are referring to is only through the help of the knowledge that is given to us. That's all. So you cannot experience...

Q: That means that the idea of world is false.

U.G.: I am not talking of the world as an illusion or a *Maya*. It is not my philosophy professors that taught me this. *Maya* means to measure. My grandmother, who was practically illiterate, told me, "Look here, *Maya* means to measure." This is the meaning of the word Maya.

There must be a point there, and in relationship with that you experience things, the world around you. So anything you experience from that point is an illusion, but the world is not an illusion. If somebody comes with a gun and he wants to shoot you what would you do? I don't know what I would do. Probably I will kill him or I will run away or I will do everything possible to protect myself. I cannot visualize what I would do in a given situation at all. So it does mean that I say that the world is an illusion but there is no way you can experience the reality of anything without using the knowledge that is given to us either by the metaphysicians or by the scientists. We all admire the scientists because their discoveries have resulted in tremendous technology, which helps us to function in this world most comfortably. That's all that they can do for us. But the same thing can be used to destroy the very thing we are trying to protect.

Q: Last question.

U.G.: Yes, sir.

Q: Generally, the purpose of philosophy is to tell people why they should do good things because they need to know, they need to have some sort of logic to do good things. Since you do not believe in philosophy, you do not believe in any cultural system. Tell me why people should do good things.

U.G.: I don't see any adequate reason why they should do anything good. While they are only concerned about doing good things, they are, all the time, doing bad things. And what they are left with is this misery of wanting to do good things. Wanting.

Q: No, you don't want them to do good things or think about good things.

U.G.: Because there are no good things and bad things for me. I am perfectly satisfied with the world as it is. The demand to bring about a change isn't there anymore.

Q: No matter how miserable it sounds?

U.G.: I don't see anything miserable there. We are responsible for the misery. Individually, there isn't a damn thing, if I may use that word...

Q: There must be something to…

U.G.: Why do you say there must be something? You see? You do something. What is it that they are doing? They are talking of a new world order, the world in transition, the world from where to where.

Q: You think this world cannot be improved at all?

U.G.: Why should it be different? It can't be any different. We being what we are I don't see any reason, and I don't believe the world can be any different. It has always been the same. I once told a friend of mine that we have not made any tremendous strides. We are not any more different from the caveman who used the jawbone of an ass to kill his neighbor, and now with the help of all these scientists, nuclear physicists, we have destructive weapons to destroy the whole thing that we have created with great care.

Q: Mr. U.G. Krishnamurti, thank you very much.

Chapter Eight

BEYOND STATUS QUO

Human nature is exactly the same. We all speak the same language whether it is English or any other language. Everybody wants one thing, that is, to be happy without one moment of unhappiness. To have pleasure without pain. It is just impossible to achieve that goal. The religious teachers from time immemorial have brainwashed us to believe that they have a teaching which will help us to make that possible. They have not succeeded, and we have fallen for that kind of a thing.

We live in hope and die in hope because we still believe that it will be possible for us to have one without the other. I say it is not possible because this living organism is involved in that demand to have permanent happiness. All sensations are short-lived. Happiness is also one sensation; pleasure is one sensation. But this living organism is interested in one basic thing: to maintain its sensitivity of the sensory activity and the nervous system. Then alone it can survive and face the rigors of living in these adverse circumstances. We have added one more problem to this living organism that it is fighting all the time: the demand to make that a permanent thing, to be happy forever. It is not possible.

The quest for permanent happiness is consuming tremendous amounts of energy. So we are not left with any energy to face the problems of our living. What is it that we can't do in this world? The idea that we should create a heaven on this planet is the one that has turned this extraordinary paradise created by nature into a hellish state.

Because we have achieved tremendous things in the field of science, and we have put man on the moon, we are going to put man on every planet. That does mean that all that we have discovered, the laws of nature, has not in any way benefitted the whole of mankind. It benefits only a negligible percentage of the people.

And so what I want to emphasize is that it is possible for us to live happily on this planet which nature has created for us. But the problem here is that we have been made to believe that the human species is created for some grander purpose other than all the other species on this planet. That's the first error that the culture has done. The second is the belief that the whole thing is created for the benefit of mankind. So we think that we have a right to enjoy whatever is there in nature for ourselves and deny the basic things for everybody. There is tremendous amount of things available for everybody on this planet.

They say that whatever nature has can feed 12 billion people without the help of modern technology. We have only 5 billion people on this planet. Why there is misery? Where there is starvation? We have to ask these basic questions and we have to get answers. Otherwise, we are heading towards disaster.

We are not ready to question the answers. We are not ready to question the solutions that are offered to us to solve the problems. There are actually no problems at all. The problem is that the solutions that have been offered to us are not really the solutions. If they were the solutions there wouldn't be any problems there at all.

So something is wrong somewhere. It is only on the individual level that an individual being can to look at these things and see the absurdity that we have made of our lives and world around us.

Q: The continued dominance of advanced industrialized nations over the world's resources is a concern to many of us. You find that the inequitable distribution of world economic resources is a very disturbing malady in the contemporary economic scene.

U.G.: The nine industrial nations are controlling the resources of the whole world. We have placed them in the seat of power and we have given them most powerful destructive weapons, and they are going to use them to see that they are not dislodged. So you and I are responsible for the situation there. We have to stop thinking about what harm or what good religion has done. The human thought reaches acme in India. It cannot go beyond. Our country has produced tremendous thinkers, tremendous philosophers.

Q: You feel that change is the essence of progress. Yet there is a lot of places yet to change. Why is this irony?

U.G.: You may talk all the time that you want a change, but when the time comes for change you will not let that have a change for the better. That is the nature of things. *Status quo* is all that is important to the culture and to the individual. It is like a crab; we are here in this hole. Something happens; it pushes out unwillingly, hesitantly, reluctantly, it moves and makes another hole and sits there until something happens and pushes. That's the way we are moving.

Q: You don't have much reverence for history when you outline the distortion and unequal distribution of means for the benefits of mankind.

U.G.: What is, after all, history? History is the memory of nations, and it is no different from your own memory. That is the most important thing. So we do not want any change there. You may talk of change. Change for your own benefit. So change for maintaining the continuity and *status quo*.

All that the human mind has invented is only to maintain its status. That is the reason why, when the time comes to change the leadership of the nations, they always pat their backs and tell themselves that a known enemy is better than an unknown friend.

Q: On the vital issue of disarmament and destruction of nuclear weapons you say that the technology is in the memory and the violence takes root in the mind.

U.G.: The root of all that wall building is very important. Every time I pass that red fort I say to myself, "Where are those people who built those things to protect themselves?" They are gone. And we have survived them all.

The time has come for us where the possibility of anybody surviving a nuclear holocaust is slim to none. But are we going to be foolish enough to destroy what we ourselves have created with such a tremendous care. That is anybody's guess. When once you have entrenched yourself and have the means of defending yourself at any cost, what we will do is anybody's guess.

I don't think we'll be that foolish to destroy everything. The superpowers have come to realize that if they tried to destroy their adversaries they will also go with them. So the terror has turned them to look towards trying to live with their adversaries. That kind of a thing has to percolate to the level of the common man.

So that is the reason why I maintain that it is not "Love thy neighbor as thyself" which we have been preaching for centuries. Brotherhood, cooperation and all that kind of a guff is nonsense. What is real is the terror that if I tried to destroy my neighbor I would go down with him. But the basic question is: how are you going to create peace through war?

What is the enemy of man? You are not ready to...I am not for a moment asking you to discard that. It's a very powerful instrument. So all philosophy does is to sharpen that instrument. That's very necessary. But it is used for purposes for which it is not intended, such as the quest for happiness, the quest for excellence, the quest for God-realization, etc., etc.

So is there any other instrument? The Roman state has created a tremendous structure of philosophical thought. Any division that is there, any frontier you create out of that division is one problem that we have to face. So is there any other instrument that we have?

I've been asking myself to not bother about seeing these religious freaks, religious buffs anymore. These religious seekers try and use another medium, and they are asking me suddenly: why have you gone public, why are you anxious to become famous? No, not at all. The radio and the television are the most powerful media through which I think I can express myself and talk to the unknown people.

Q: Well Mr. Krishnamurti, first of all we have to analyze the wonderful world called happiness...in quest of it...every human species is always in the wrong. Can you tell us: what is this happiness?

U.G.: You see, you use the word "the quest for happiness." You may not agree with me but when we use that word happiness it is no different from any other sensual activity. As a matter of fact all the experiences, however extraordinary they may be, are all in the area of sensuality. That is one major problem that we are facing today.

Somewhere along the line the human species experienced this self-consciousness for the first time. And it separated the human species from the rest of the species on this planet. I don't even know if there is any such a thing as evolution, but we are made to believe there is such a thing as evolution.

But it was at that time that thought took its birth. And thought in its birth, in its origin, in its content, in its expression and in its action is very fascist. When I use the word fascist I do not use it in the political sense, but rather in the way that it controls and shapes our thinking and our actions. So it is a very protective mechanism. It has no doubt helped us to be what we are today. It has helped us in the high-tech and technology, and it has made our lives very comfortable. And also it has become possible for us to discover the laws of nature.

But thought is a very protective mechanism. It is interested in survival, and that is opposed fundamentally to the functioning of this living organism. We are made to believe that there is such a thing as mind, but there is no such thing as your mind or my mind.

The society or culture or whatever you want to call it has created us all solely and wholly for the main purpose of maintaining its continuity and its *status quo*. And at the same time it has also created the idea, given us the idea, that there is such a thing as individual. And, actually, this is the conflict between the two—the idea of an individual and the impossibility of functioning as an individual separate from and distinct from the totality of man's thoughts and experiences.

Q: The happiness depends on the thought one gets. Yes, we can do as we think, but who makes us think in a particular way?

U.G.: Here at this point I would like to emphasize that the thoughts are not self-generated and spontaneous. I would even go one step further: is there any such thing as thought? The very question arises because we assume there is such a thing as thought, and that we can separate ourselves from thought and look at it. What we see or look at is *about* thought and not thought itself.

What is thought? The question arises only because of the assumption that there is such a thing as thought. But we use what we call thought to achieve our goals, spiritual or material. Thought to me is matter. The culture in which we are functioning places spiritual goals on a higher level than the materialistic goals. The instrument which we are using is matter. And so all of the spiritual goals are materialistic in their value.

And this is the conflict that is going on there: in this process, the totality of man's experiences created what we call a separate identity and a separate mind. But actually if you want to experience anything with your own body or your own experiences you have no way of experiencing it without the use of knowledge that is passed on to us.

So thought, in other words, is memory. But we have been made to believe that human beings are created for a nobler and grander purpose than the other species on this planet. And it is that which is responsible for us thinking that the whole thing, the whole creation, is created for the benefit of man.

Everything that is born out of thought is destructive. And so anything we discover—the laws of nature or whatever you want to call it—are used by us only for destructive purposes. And while it is true that we have discovered quite a few of nature's laws the theories are constantly changing.

Q: But one thing...cannot at least attempts to make this thought or to define this thought process, as constructive or positive, at least based on your own experience?

U.G.: Thought is not the instrument for achieving anything other than the goals set before us by our culture or society. The basic problem we have to face today is that the cultural input, or what society has placed before us as the goal for all of us to reach and attain, is the enemy of this living organism. That is the battle that is going on there. Thought can only create problems. It cannot help us to solve any problems.

Q: Then is it desirable to be thoughtless?

U.G.: What I am saying is not a thoughtless state. Even the invention of what is called a thoughtless state placed before us by many spiritual teachers as a goal to be reached is created by thought. So that it can, in pursuing what it calls a thoughtless state, guarantee that the thought can maintain its own continuity. So whatever we experience in this process of achieving the goal of a thoughtless state, these experiences fortify the very thing that we are trying to be free from.

Q: Don't you think for every action of ours, whether it is thought, or any action of ours, there is a reaction, if not immediately, at some later time?

U.G.: It is a thought that invented the cause and effect. There may not be any such a thing as cause but every event is an individual, independent event. We link up all those events and try to create this story of our lives. But actually every event is an independent event. If we accept the fact that every event is an independent event in our lives it creates a tremendous problem of maintaining what we call the identity.

Identity is the most important factor in our lives. Through the constant use of memory, which is also thought, we are able to maintain this identity. This constant use of memory or identity or whatever you call it is consuming tremendous amounts of energy and leaves us with no energy to deal with the problems of our living.

Is there any other way that we can free ourselves from this identity except through the constant use of the identity? As I said, thought can only create problems. It cannot help us to solve the problems. We are sharpening this instrument only through dialectical thinking; that is, about thinking itself. That's all that is there. All philosophies help us to sharpen this instrument, and that is very essential for us to survive in this world; but it cannot help us.

The goals that we have placed before ourselves are unachievable through the help of this thought. And as you said, the quest for happiness is impossible because there is no such thing as permanent happiness. There are moments of happiness, there are moments of unhappiness. But the demand to be in a permanent state of happiness is the enemy of this body, because this body is interested in maintaining its sensitivity of the sensory perceptions, and also the sensitivity of the nervous system. That is very essential for the survival of this body.

If we use that instrument for achieving the impossible goal of permanent happiness, the sensitivity of this body is destroyed. And so it is rejecting all that we are interested in: permanent happiness and permanent pleasure. So we are not going to succeed in that attempt to be in a permanent state of happiness.

Q: Right. The instrument for this thought, is it the intellect? But we have to solve problems from this intellect. And how to sharpen it? From whose help?

U.G.: Through repetitive process we are sharpening that instrument. In the same process of this repetitive thing we are using tremendous amounts of energy. It is limited to achieve only what we consider to be of materialistic value. If we use it to achieve our spiritual goals, then it is not possible for us to function sanely and intelligently.

It does not mean that I am preaching a materialistic philosophy or any such thing. This thought is not intended for achieving spiritual goals such as the quest for permanence or the quest for permanent pleasure; or even finding out the significance of life, the meaning of life or the purpose of life.

Q: Mr. Krishnamurti, we have been familiar with this theory of birth and death, karma, action/reaction, something we bring along with us as a bank balance. And then we spend something, and carry forward to the next birth, or whatever it is. How far do you subscribe to this? Are you opposed to this?

U.G.: I am not opposing the theory of karma, reincarnation. But I am questioning the very foundation of that belief. There is reincarnation for those who believe in reincarnation. There is no reincarnation for those who do not believe in it. But is there any such thing as reincarnation similar to the laws of nature, like gravity? My answer would be no. So it doesn't matter whether you believe or not believe in reincarnation.

If one is interested in finding out for himself and by himself, and resolve this problem of reincarnation, get an answer for this oft-repeated question "Is there any such thing as reincarnation?" you have to ask this fundamental question: what is there now you think will reincarnate?

Now, is there anything there? Is there any such thing as a soul? Is there any such thing as "I"? Is there any such thing as a psyche? Whatever you see there and whatever you experience there is created by the knowledge we have of that. So if you see the self, it is created only by the knowledge we have of that self. If you are lucky enough to be free from the totality of knowledge, not only the knowledge we have of the self, reincarnation and all kinds of things, then is it possible for you to experience any center, any "I", any self, any soul? So to me the "I" is nothing but a first-person singular pronoun. I do not see any center, any self there. And so the whole idea of reincarnation is built on the foundation of our belief.

Q: What is it that makes one a great person in due course of time? And what is it that keeps a person essentially stagnant in his mental process? Do you advocate some kind of evolvement or fate or inherent gift?

U.G.: We have always been curious and interested in finding out why a child is born with a deformity. And it was a very interesting theory evolved by the human mind at that time to explain away and give comfort; to face the situation that we have such people in our midst.

But now it is possible for us, in light of what they are doing in genetic research and microbiology, to correct deformities created by nature that we attributed either to nature or to the evils that we collected in our previous lives. It is materially irrelevant. It is now possible through the help of genetic engineering to correct the deformities for which even nature has no way of explaining.

Why do we still want to attribute this to something terrible that we did in our previous lives? That kind of a belief comes very handy to us. We have in our midst today a tremendous amount of suffering, poverty, starvation and degradation.

It is very comforting for us to believe that suffering is there because they did something terrible in their past life. That is no answer to give to solve this problem that is very essential for us. It is neither spiritual nor human. In the name of doing something human for your fellow being, we have perpetuated in human depth and maintained the continuity of this. That will only help us to look the other side and not deal with the problem which is demanding the answers from every thinking man this world today.

Q: So Mr. Krishnamurti, Mr. J. Krishnamurti, he was always emphasizing on one fact: that nobody requires a guru. And that he would not like to be a guru for anybody. That is what he was claiming and then continuously saying until the end. According to you, what is the role of the guru in paving the way for this fundamental change?

U.G.: I think that's the wrong word that we use these days. All those spiritual gurus we have in the market, selling shoddy goods and exploiting the gullibility and credibility of the people. A guru is one who tells you to throw away all crutches we have been made to believe are essential for our survival. The guru tells you: throw them away. And don't replace them with fancy crutches or even computerized crutches. You can walk. And if you fall you will rise and walk.

Such is the man who weakens the tradition considered to be the real guru and not those who are selling those shoddy goods in the marketplace today. It is a business, you see? It has become a holy business for people. I am not condemning anything. But as long as you depend upon somebody for solving your problems you remain helpless. And so this is exploited by the people who actually do not have the answers for these problems, but give you some sort of a comforter. And people are satisfied with these comforters and fall for that kind of a thing instead of dealing with the problem for themselves and by themselves.

Q: What do you suggest as the inertia for the human misery, the deprivation, the kind of suffering everyone on this planet is facing these days, of their financial position or their benefits of having this planet. Everyone is having this wanting, something to seek always.

U.G.: As we started this discussion with this quest for happiness. It is all that anybody, whether he is a Russian or an American or an African or Indian, is interested in. But as I said, it is impossible to achieve that goal because of the physical problem that is involved in achieving that goal.

It is assumed that the West is materialist and it is looking to the East for spiritual guidance. That is not really true. If you live for a longer period in the West you will realize that those who are interested in these spiritual matters are not really the people who are guiding the destinies of this world.

What was responsible for this sudden interest in spiritual matters? And they are looking to the East for a substitute for drugs. That gave them a sort of experience, and they were not satisfied by repeating those experiences. They were looking around for varieties of religious experiences, whether they go here, India, or to Japan or China, they are attracted to these things because of the new language and new techniques.

The fact of the matter is that when once you have everything that you can reasonably ask for in this world, when all the material needs are taken care of naturally the question arises, "Is that all?" And once you pose that question to yourself—"Is that all?" —a tremendous market for this kind of a business is created; a holy business. And they are exploiting the gullibility and credibility of people, not helping them to resolve the basic problem, the human problem. It is not that simple.

So we have to ask questions over and over again. And all the questions that we are asking are born out of the answers we already have. It never occurs to us to ask ourselves why we keep asking the questions when we already have the answers given to us by the sages, saints and saviors of mankind. But we forget to realize that the answers that they have given are responsible for the tragedy of mankind. We don't question them. If we question the answers we would be questioning the teachers.

If humanity is to be saved from the chaos of its own making it has to be free from the saviors of mankind. That does not mean you will destroy everything, but you will have to ask questions not born out of the answers. We already have, but is there any answer...that's all. There it stops and the solution is there for us.

Q: So the quest continues unabated. Thank you very much.

U.G.: Thank you sir.

Chapter Nine

THERE IS NOTHING
TO BE FREE FROM

There is no such thing as spontaneity. What we call spontaneous is really not spontaneous because if there is any such a thing as a spontaneous response to the stimulus out *there* there is no space between the two, there is no division between the two. The stimulus and response, you see, is a unitary movement. So there is no way you can say that this is a spontaneous response to something you are confronted with.

You mentioned at the very beginning that you had an opportunity to read that book and when you read a book of that kind, even then it is not for the first time you are reading that book. So when you repeat what is there on the title "Disquieting Conversations with a man called U.G." it has already created a disquiet in you because there is a reference point there; there is no way you can listen to or see or hear or smell anything because you, what you call "you", must be there. You is the one which is born out of the memory, the identity. The cultural input is all that is there, otherwise there is no way you can respond to anything.

Q: Let me just clarify that. There is no absolute spontaneity because however anybody responds to the situation is conditioned upon the accumulation of...

U.G.: ...knowledge we have of things. And the knowledge is born out of the memory that is put in there, you know? So there is no such thing as having to know something otherwise there is no way you can experience anything.

What you call your experiences, actually and factually, cannot be your experience, because all of our experiences are born out of the experiences that are passed on to us from generation to generation. So even when you are looking at that fireplace out *there*, unless you know what it is you have *no way* of looking at it without telling yourself that it is a fireplace and that's a fire. I don't know if I'm making myself clear?

Q: I'm going to try and stay with you here and continue to refine this so that it's understandable. If that's all true then for the most part we are not making free-will decisions, are we?

U.G.: Absolutely not. There is no way you can say that you have freedom of action or free will. Metaphysically you can explain, logically you can establish a point of view, but actually there is no freedom of action because all the actions are born out of our thinking, and the thinking is born out of the thoughts that are put in there. And I question the very thoughts and thinking.

I say that there are no thoughts and there is no thinking there at all. Thought is nothing but memory, so it's a recognition of what *we know*. We know that is fire and we know that is a gentleman. I know that this is a microphone. I know that is a tape recorder, so the word tape recorder is the identity here. You may not accept what I am saying. So what you call U.G. is, in one frame, the microphone; in another frame, a tape recorder; in another frame, an audio cassette or video cassette as the case may be. It is a limited instrument.

So there is an illusion or an impression that there is a person or that there is one who is saying all these things. Each one is an independent thing. So the identity can be maintained only by assuming that it is the same thing that is saying all these things. I don't know if I make myself clear?

Q: Well, to put it in to the context for our listeners, as somebody hearing this, to understand I'm getting little bits of it, I've also tried to study some of the philosophies from books and teachers of the East that you are radically departed from, so I don't know where we are going to go with this, other than…

U.G.: Say call myself a person who is radically departed from anything but they are in a very strange position in the East, especially in India. Those who come to see me, all of them are religious people. Even Pontiffs come to see me, philosophers of all and every kind, but for some reason they are not able to brush me aside for the simple reason that they are still trying, struggling, to put me to that framework of what is passed on to them. So my answer to all those questions is: that's all that they can do.

Either they have to reject me, saying that all this is nonsense, or accept me because they have succeeded in fitting me into that framework which is the only thing that they have. So they always have to put a sort-of label on me, call me a guru, call me anti-guru, you are a cynic, you are this, you are that. Otherwise there is no way they can succeed in fitting me into any framework.

That's what you are also doing, that's what everybody here is doing. If you don't do that, the you as you know yourself, the you as you experience yourself is not there. So you are interested in adding more and more to that, and maintain and give continuity to that, otherwise you are in a very dangerous situation, so you have to *know* and fit what I am saying into the framework of the known there.

So as I was saying awhile ago to him in the car, I asked my friend, he has been with me for 25 years. And they all ask me questions, even after 25 years. It's amazing that they ask me the same questions. So one day I asked him, "You have known me for 25 years, probably 26 years now. If somebody asks you a question, 'What the hell you are doing with that man called U.G.?' what would you say?'"

So the answer to that question, if there is any answer, is that everything that is going on there mustn't be there. If I say mustn't be there the word is a very misleading word. Any movement that is there trying to understand or say that this is the same thing as all the other teachers said, this is not the same thing as all the other great teachers said, this is something absolute rubbish. So any movement that is there indicates that you have not understood what this man has been saying, and there is no way you can understand because all that I'm saying—when once that movement is not there—there is no need for you to understand. There is nothing to understand. This is all that I'm saying. That's the reason why I say you always ask the question how? How? How? The one thing that should happen to the literature, English, all languages, is that the word *how* should be removed from the languages.

Q: How about why?

U.G.: The why is also the variation on the same how. By asking that question you want to know. So by adding more and more to what you already know, you are making it difficult for you to put yourself...

And any word I use is a misleading word, to be in a situation where there is nothing to understand...you don't even tell yourself, "There is nothing to understand." You don't even tell yourself that I don't know what he is saying, you know? So when once that movement is not there there is no need for you to say anything to yourself or say anything to anybody else because what you are left with is something that you will never know and you have no way of knowing, and it can never, never become part of that movement. That is all that I am doing there, trying to add more and more and maintain its continuity.

Q: I think I understand and in this moment would strive to create a new place. Starting fresh. Now I know that's going to be difficult because I'm a creature of 51 years of learning, and during this time in an attempt to know myself or discover or realize what this journey in this body is about I've realized a lot of the stuff I've learned, I've had to unlearn because it didn't serve me. Now where are we headed? Why am I here and why are you here? Ok.

U.G.: You said that you are trying to unlearn but the instrument that you have to use to free yourself from what you have known is the same instrument.

Q: My mind? Or brain-mind complex?

U.G.: The brain is not interested. The brain is not even listening to what I am saying. As long as the listener is there, the question of listening or not listening or the invented thing called the art of listening, all that guff, is part of that.

But this mechanism that is operating there, the brain or whatever you want to call it, is not involved in translating what is being said here. It doesn't even know that this is the English language. It's like the tape recorder, it is recording everything. The tape recorder does not know that it is recording anything at all. It does not know that what is being said happens to be the English language or some other language. So that is the way this living organism is operating. Nobody listens to anything, you see? The listener is the one who is listening. As long as the listener is listening his only interest is to give continuity to that listener.

Q: So why are we here, U.G.? And what is our purpose if it's not to accumulate experience? Some would say our purpose here is to be fulfilled and happy even though we struggle as a society...why are we here?

U.G.: That living organism is living, a living thing would never ask those questions. I always give a very, very, very silly answer. We are here because our parents made love. I don't know...we are committing the same folly, you see? I have brought into this world so many children so that is not really what is there behind this basic question "why we are here?" because you think that there is something more interesting to do than what you are doing. And something more purposeful there must be in our lives than this dull, dreary, drab existence of ours, doing the same thing, thinking the same thoughts, feeling the same feelings, experiencing the same experiences. If you don't "do" you are not there, so you have to continue to experience the same thing over and over and over again. That's the only way you can maintain the continuity of yourself. You understand?

So that is not the instrument that you can use to unlearn yourself. You don't have to unlearn anything. The question "How to unlearn?" does not at all arise. There is nothing there to unlearn because you don't know a thing about what is put in there.

Q: Did you personally have some realization at some point in time about all this that you're conditioned and what you learned...

U.G.: Don't use that word conditioning because it has certain psychological connotations.

Q: What's a better word?

U.G.: The living organism is conditioned. It has to be conditioned because it's such a mechanical organism that there is no way of considering the pros and cons, the right and wrong, the good and bad, this division is totally absent there. So it's so mechanical that's it's not interested in asking those questions.

Q: I was asking what happened to you.

U.G.: The conditioning you are talking about is bound to be there, it will continue to be there, as long as you want to uncondition yourself and place before yourself an idea of an unconditioned being, unconditioned mind. You don't realize this intent of our thought. To free yourself from conditioning and to function as an unconditioned individual you are conditioning yourself in a different way.

There's no way that you can avoid this process of conditioning, and it will continue to do that as long as you want to free yourself from the conditioning. To me there is no way you can function as an unconditioned individual. But this conditioning here that is born with this living organism is necessary for its survival, absolutely necessary. So this is not interested in freeing itself from the conditioned way in which it is functioning. I don't know if this makes any sense...?

Q: No, no, no. I'm hearing what you're saying. And any attempt to uncondition is another form of conditioning.

U.G.: Any intent on your part to unlearn yourself is also a learning process. So you are stuck with this....in such a situation there is no way you can resolve the problem by yourself or for yourself. So if you seek help from somebody else, he will put you on a merry-go-round because he himself has not resolved the problem, for and by himself.

Q: What would you say to the organisms striving for an attempt to have some peace in their life?

U.G.: It is a peaceful organism. I maintain that the body does not want to know anything. It does not want to learn anything. So whatever you are interested in is not in helping this living organism but trying to resolve the problems created by that mechanism that is put in there by our culture or society.

Q: Alright, I'm with you on this. Because I feel this and I know some other people who feel this—that we are acting in response to a construct that we have learned, that we are stuck in this whole attempt to survive at some level based on what people have told us, rather than just hanging out.

U.G.: That is true. The problem is to be free from the fantasy that through *that* you'll be able to resolve this problem. All this effort on the part of us to free ourselves from the fantasy of transformation, or radical transformation or something like enlightenment and all that kind of nonsense that is passed on to us from generation to generation, is a monumental waste of energy.

And so there is not a thing that you can do about it. You see, any word I use is born out of this duality. I don't mean the duality in the sense that the Atman, Brahman, God, soul and all that kind of thing. The language is a busy movement in this living organism. It is a unitary movement, it cannot separate itself from anything that is happening out there or inside here. And to divide the thing and say "out there" and "in here" is also a divisive movement there. Divisive movement is not part of this living organism.

It is not interested in peace at all. It is a very peaceful living organism, and so that idea that you have a peaceful state of mind, or a peaceful entity, is the one that is disturbing the peace that is already there. So all that you are doing to create a peaceful mind, or a peaceful way of living, is rejected by this living organism because that is not the part of this living organism.

Q: Okay. If, from your perspective, people would be living in a more natural way, without the conditioning, how would it be here? You know? How would we act in that place?

U.G.: It will not be your action or my action. It is not an action which is born out of your thinking. All our actions are born out of thinking and that thinking is to use these thoughts to free yourself from something, you see? So to free yourself from something will never, never help you to free yourself from that because it is that movement that is disturbing the whole thing, you know?

Q: Do you have any focus or purpose in your teaching or your dialogue?

U.G.: Now we happen to be here and you are interviewing me. And my interest is to focus, spotlight, that all that you are doing to free yourself from something that does not exist there is the one thing that is keeping you where you are.

I can say that there is nothing there to be free from. So it hit me like a lightning; that's the only word that I can use. There is nothing there to be free from. It doesn't matter what you want to be free from. There is nothing there to be free from. So wanting to be free from this, wanting to be free from that, you have hundreds of different thing you want to be free from. So when something hits you that there is nothing there to be free from, it can hit you so hard that you won't know what is happening there. You will never know what you are left with. There is nobody who is talking here.

There is nobody who is listening. Are you listening? I don't listen. You see, when he is saying something, asking questions in what is supposed to be the English language, this listening mechanism does not listen to what you are saying as English language. It is not even translating.

Q: So who's translating?

U.G.: There is no translator. Your demand for an answer is the one that brings out what is there—the printout I call it—from the computer that is there. And if there is no answer there at all for that question, if there is no information there in the computer, it does not even say that the data is not formed. Like when the computers are searching; you ask a question, you put a question there, searching it says, but here it doesn't even say to itself that it is searching.

If there is any info that is there in the computer it comes out as an answer to you, but actually there is nobody who is giving answers. It may sound mystifying, but it is not mystifying here. What is going on is a conversation between the questioner and the one you think is giving the answers. The questions are yours and if I say the questions are yours the questions are not yours. The questions are born out of the answers that you already have. Otherwise there can't be any questions at all. So the answers you are getting are also from the answers you already have.

I recognize it may sound very mystifying but it's not mystifying. That's the way this living organism, the human body, is functioning. At no time do I translate what you are saying into the language that I know. The answers are also coming out of this computer, whatever you want to call it. It is your problem and not the problem of this which is just listening to what you are saying.

Q: Well, we seem to be trying to define this organism, you, and this organism, me, here.

U.G.: This division is artificially made. There's no questioner and there's nobody who is giving the answers. And so we are two persons making some noises, you know? Whatever may be the reasons why we are doing this ... but the translation of that or the fitting these ... we are creating, if I may put it this way, space between these two notes. That is what we are taught and that's the language. And so I have been taught how to create the space between the two notes, and that's music also. Otherwise there is no music at all—it just noise, like the barking of that dog. And so we are taught how to space these two notes and the tune which we are using says that this is English, not French, not Italian.

Q: The difference is in the vibrations of the sound.

U.G.: In the vibrations of the sound, yes.

Q: Because at one point you didn't know English or I didn't know English. We learned it.

U.G.: If I knew some other language I would try to fit these noises into the framework and tell myself that this also a language. The fact that we recognize the noises as French or Italian or some other language we do not know of means that there is a movement here trying to fit all those noises into a framework that you already know.

Q: Getting back to the question that you said awhile back: "Why am I here?" Your response was that my mother and father had sexual relationship with each other...coming together in a biological way to create another life form. Now that we're here...

U.G.: So this living organism is interested in only two things: to survive and to reproduce. And we have introduced the element of thought into this sex element also, which is a very natural basic thing. That is why it has become possible for humans to have sex at any time they want—otherwise we would be like all the other animals. And sex is just there to reproduce one life. That's all.

So once the thought is introduced into the whole functioning of the human organism it is bound to be a pleasure movement. That's the reason why it always make frivolous statements. Just as you can have varieties of fruit you can also have varieties of girls and varieties of boys; because there is no difference between the two. The other part of my statement might not be socially acceptable because it will create social problems and a whole lot of problems that are associated with it. Basically, essentially, it's the same.

Q: What are the problems that you are talking about that it will create?

U.G.: The children, properties, security, the *status quo* and the tradition. What is tradition, after all? The unwillingness on our part to change with the changing things.

[Recording abruptly ends]

Chapter Ten

THERE IS NOTHING ORIGINAL

Q: Why do you think people need guru figures? Why do they turn to all these gurus?

U.G.: I have very often said this and I want to repeat it again. It's the Oriental countries; that's the culture in which we were brought up. And there were no escapes for us in those days. Religion was the only escape for people.

But in the West, why they are falling for all these gurus that come? It is that once you have everything that you can reasonably ask for this basic question springs up—pops up—in us and we ask ourselves and others: is that all? We are not ready to accept that's all, you see? We have been brainwashed to believe that we are materialistic in our thinking and our way of life; and they have unfortunately superimposed on that what is called the spiritual life, and we have all been persuaded for generations to follow or pursue the spiritual life.

Unfortunately, the value system we have in this world is modeled after the spiritual teachers and their walks of life. And they have placed before us the model of a perfect being. Nature is creating perfect species, but perfect species are quite different from perfect beings. That is why there is this suffering, this misery.

We accept, once that is the model for us, that the way we are living and feeling and thinking just doesn't fit into us. And that turned us all into neurotic individuals.

Q: Well, not all of us I suppose. But still certainly there is that element in every seeker.

U.G.: Yes, but that applies to every mode of thinking, not necessarily the religious thinking of the mind. You might not agree and your listeners probably will reject when I say, and I say with great emphasis, that thought in its very birth and its content, in its expression and in its action, is fascist. It may be quite different from the political ideology called fascism, but it wants to control everything.

One basic demand of us all is that we believe. The need to believe things is exploited by the spiritual teachers, past, present and probably the teachers to be born. They force us to believe in what they are saying. And the political ideologies are exactly the same. All the political ideologies are nothing but the warty outgrowth of religion.

U.G. Krishnamurti

Q: You yourself have had some kind of enlightenment experience, haven't you? I think it was in 1967 in Switzerland. What do you mean by the word "enlightenment"? What were you freed from?

U.G.: I am freed from the demand to be enlightened. It was there, naturally, because I was born in a religious atmosphere superimposed on that theosophical atmosphere. I was surrounded by the holy men all through my life, especially in the formative years. And I found, rather I was intrigued, when I discovered that there was a dichotomy in their lives. What they preached was one thing, and the teachings and the preachings didn't produce the results. They blamed the followers saying the teaching is alright—something is wrong with you.

So I said to myself, "Something is wrong with the teaching of these people." If the teaching doesn't produce results then something is wrong with the teacher as well. But then the sentimentality comes into the picture, and we cannot so easily brush aside the teachers.

And the teachers there around me were the imitators of the great teachers that mankind is supposed to have produced. And this was really my problem, you see? I didn't call them this, that or the other, but why am I interested in enlightenment? Because I was brought up in that atmosphere, the be-all and end-all of our existence was to attain enlightenment. And then when once the whole traditional background went out of my system I switched over to psychology, to science, to modern contributions of the thinkers of our day. And I didn't discover anything original there.

So I go to the extent of saying that there is nothing original in anybody. I can say that the thoughts I think are not my own, the feelings I feel are not my own and the experiences I experience are not my own because all my experiences are born out of the thinking process. So there is nothing original. I have a friend who is one of the top film directors, and is also the biographer of my book, and I tell him always, "Don't call the source 'you're always original'."

I discovered in my own way, and I still maintain, that this human body is nothing but an extraordinary computer with a tremendous, unparalleled, innate, inborn intelligence. And the intellect that we have acquired through repetitive process, through study, through this, that and the others is no match for that. I'm not here to give a talk but let me say what I want to say. And so I somehow—it hit me one day like a lightning or an earthquake that there is no such a thing as enlightenment at all, and why the hell have I been pursuing this, wanting this?

And everything that is there in the book I have, through the help of my own thought and experience, anything that is there you can experience. Is there anything I can experience that I do not know?

So it occurred to me, and still I maintain, that what you do not know you cannot experience. What we know is always the second-hand, third-hand knowledge that is passed on to us from generation to generation. And then that's switched on to me and put me in a situation where I wanted to want something that nobody else wanted. Everything I wanted, you see, was what they wanted me to want. Is there anything that I want other than what they wanted it to be?

Then I found there was nothing that I wanted to want other than that, than what they wanted me to want. But it never occurred to me that that is also a want, not to want what they wanted me to want. And so it hit me so hard like an earthquake or a lightning bolt, and finished the whole thing.

And what happened? Has anything happened? I don't even know. So I am certain that there is no such thing as enlightenment at all, and this certainty that dawned on me is a result of a fleshing out of everything that everybody said and experienced before me. It left me with the extraordinary way this body is functioning.

So people always ask me the question: "Are you enlightened or not?" To me, there is no such thing as enlightenment at all—anybody who claims he is an enlightened man can set up a holy business. This is unfair and it's a tragedy for those who follow such people. And at the same time I'm not interested in condemning those people who have set up holy businesses to enlighten other people. It's not my business, you see? They have to find out for themselves and by themselves that they are all taking them for a ride, just the way I found myself that I was misled, misguided and ended up a misspent man.

So it's my not my interest to free them. In that sense, I am not a missionary to free them from their teachers. There is a demand obviously, and they are suffering because of that demand.

I don't know. Try and buy one Rolls-Royce car. You see? It's not a joke. 336 Rolls-Royce's is a joke. You know those people who give, denying themselves the basic things for themselves? It is an easy way of living for the gurus.

But everybody is caught up in something or the other, the civil liberties or political ideology or religious ideology or you name it. As I said at the very beginning: we have to believe and we need to believe.

Q: We also need to understand, don't we? There is a very basic desire to understand the world. Do you feel that your message is helping people to understand or is it just lulling them in some way?

U.G.: No, no, no. You see, this was my question: the demand to understand myself and the world around me. When once the demand to bring about a change in you isn't there the demand to change the world is also not there. And what is the instrument that I am using to understand myself and to understand the world around me? I said to myself, this is not the instrument that *can* help me to understand, that *will* help me to understand. And there is no other instrument. So...

Q: This is a dark message...

U.G.: No, it is not a dark message. When you face the reality of the situation that this instrument is not the instrument at all, and there is no other instrument, there is nothing to understand. You see? But I never said to myself that there is nothing to understand. This finished the whole thing. And I did not get up on a platform and proclaim, "Come, heed people and listen to me. I have found something, I have understood something." I'm a teacher combining all the other teachers that existed before me, finished. That was the end of it, you see?

So, when people come to see me I just point out: "Look here, you see I can discuss any subject from this Eastern divinity, I have opinions on everything in this world." At the same time I know that opinions are no more valid than the opinions of the fellow that is sweeping the floor there or collecting the garbage. See, we think that here is this religious man or enlightened man; his opinions are very important and they will help us to understand something. But as far as I'm concerned, my opinions are no more important than the opinions of anybody in this world.

Chapter Eleven

RARE DISCUSSION
WITH DAVID BOHM

B: Well, perhaps I could say…I think I met you about the beginning of last year, and then I went off to America, and when I came back, I heard that you had some unusual experiences. We were very busy at that time, so we naturally couldn't get to see you, but perhaps we could start discussing on that line.

U.G.: I guess, but they were indeed very unusual for me, and instead of telling you how I got into that it would be perhaps better for me to describe what actually I got into, you see?

I got into a new state of being, as it were. Mr. L. was here at the time, and witnessed the whole of changes in me. It came about in quite an unexpected way. One day, you probably have heard this before; let me go over it all over again. One day I was lying here, on the same sofa, and suddenly I found my body was missing, you know? And then I opened my eyes and looked at myself, the body was intact, so was my eyes. And then I found that my body was missing. Well I didn't pay any attention to that. The next day B. was here for lunch with a few of his friends; I told him that yesterday I found my body missing, and it hasn't come back to me yet.

And then another Sunday, there was a man here who practices homeopathy, and he said oh no, something is terribly with you. It's something like the separation of body. Let me go and get some homeopathic pills. He went and got some pills, but I felt that it's something more than separation of body.

A series of changes took place one day. I found that my head suddenly became very soft, like in milk, and then the next day I found that my vision changed. And then my listening, and then my taste changed, and I found all my senses, five senses, started functioning in a different kind of way. The whole thing was so puzzling to me. I didn't know what it was, but yet somehow the whole thing became so panicky to me, I didn't realize what it was all about.

All these changes took almost a week to take place. One day the eyes, another day the ears, the taste, and the following the day skin, and the fifth day I don't remember what happened. On the sixth day, I was sitting there again, and I felt, all of a sudden, the life was simply ebbing out of me. And then I called her, and said that I feel as if I'm going to die. I had come to the end of my life.

I always said that if something happens to me hand over this body to one of the hospitals. Don't bother about what to do with my body. And then she found me. The whole body turned blue, I was terribly shaking, and I felt as if life was ebbing out of me, from every part of my body. I couldn't sit there and stretch myself.

But then, the whole thing was sinking inside of me, as it were, like a vacuum cleaner—sucked out. And then, you see, I was in a peculiar kind of state. There was a terrible pain in my head, pain all over my body, and then the last thing…

This is very difficult for me to go over all these things, but by way of introduction it is very necessary to explain what happened, because all my memories are not now fading out. It's very difficult for me to recall with vividness what happened to me. But I vaguely remember. Then suddenly I felt, to use a simile, like the aperture of a camera, trying to close itself, and something in me trying to keep it open; and then again it was forcing itself to close down. I tried to keep it open but suddenly it closed—this self. And what happened afterwards I didn't know but after nearly an hour and a half I came out of this.

The whole thought completely disappeared, you see? I felt as if I had no past at all of any kind, like I was waking up from a deep slumber as if for the first time in my life. It was a clean slate. And then I didn't sleep that night at all, because it was a very disturbed night. The next morning, on the seventh day, I woke again as if I was waking up for the first time in my life; and from then on there were a series of situations for me.

Then the next day I was sitting here, and suddenly the body started vibrating with tremendously terrific vibrations. I didn't know what to do. I couldn't control the vibrations, there were so terrific. And wave after wave, it started coming up from here to the head, and these waves were trying to escape through the brain, or something through the head, and this went on for nearly a half an hour—wave after wave, wave after wave, wave after wave, with greater and greater speed. Then I couldn't control myself, yet I tried to hold on.

I called her and said, "Something is happening to me." And she didn't know what it was. She said, "You can't do it by any words, always we have to put up with this." And it went on for half an hour, like that. Then I went to my room and stretched myself on the bed, and the whole night, this terrific wave after wave, like the ocean waves, moved through me, starting from here, from foot to head, it went on the whole night. I don't know what it was. I didn't bother to do anything.

But then I suddenly realized that there is something more to it than the way I am affecting these things. But anyway, let me wait and see. And then the whole of this body, I couldn't rest myself on the bed, turn myself this way, that way, and it was such a terrific pain here; not only here, the whole head was painful, you know?

And then from that moment onward my awareness started changing all of a sudden. By daylight, I was in a peculiar kind of awareness. The awareness of things outside and the awareness of things inside. That was the beginning, you see? And then I go for a walk, and I see the things, and I don't know what they are. And I look at her, and I don't know who she is.

B: You can't name her?

U.G.: No, no. But it started this way. The naming process was not there. She went out of this room and she's out of my consciousness. She has been with me for 5 or 6 years, every day, as long as she is here, as long I am looking at her she is here. But the moment she goes outside, she doesn't exist for me at all. The noises she makes in the other room were not in any way related to her. Something totally unrelated, these two things. And then these kinds of bewildering things continued for days and days, and this pain in the head.

And then I felt that some kind of a change was going on inside my body. This was some kind of awareness, because every cell in my body, every gland in my body was hit by something, something like lightning. And all the cells, every part of my brain, were undergoing some kind of a transformation, as it were. Every organ in my body, I felt, was undergoing some kind of change. It went on for two or three weeks. But I didn't pay any attention.

And then my breathing changed. Suddenly I felt that the air was escaping through here. I would breathe in, and suddenly I felt that it was escaping through some part here. I looked at it, no hole here; but at the same time it was escaping as if it was here. Then B. came in and said, "Look here, old chap. This is not a funny thing you got into." He is very well-read in the Hindu philosophy, mysticism, and yoga. He's a very well-read chap, and he lives with the Hindu monks. He said, "You have come into an extraordinary state of being, similar to that of the religious teachers." Don't treat it very lightly. But I didn't pay any attention.

So although I made purposes to philosophy, I taught Indian philosophy, I lived with monks for seven years. It never occurred to me that this could be the thing which I wanted when I was young. I worked hard and hard, and then I told him, "Maybe it is so. I don't know."

Then I set out to go to New York, the beauty, the grandeur, the center of New York. I thought I was going towards there, and suddenly, if this is what you say it is, I find myself in a God-forbidden, devil-forsaken place. Then it was something, as it were, in me. There was nothing there inside of me. And this is what you have been asking for, this is not that. That was only an image that you built for yourself, but this is actually the thing.

I said to myself, "Indeed I am playing with some kind of a dynamite." I didn't want this kind of thing. Anyway I can't do anything about this, I have to stay with this, I told myself. And then these different things continued for weeks and weeks. Everything that I looked at, the word didn't come into my mind. I look at a rose, and I then have to ask, "What is that flower?" And she says, "Rose." And we take a few steps more, and I ask her the question again. What is that? It's a rose. Like a baby. What's a matter with me? I forgot everything! Everything I look at was like the tape recorder there.

And the question arises: what is that? So then I had to ask again. These kinds of things went on for months and months and months like this. And then I said to myself, "What is the point in asking these questions?" You see a flower, you forget it. It is not even a flower to me; what it is no one knows. So why should you ask yourself, "What is that?" What does it matter whether it is a flower or a tree or a monkey or a donkey? It doesn't matter at all. Why do you go out questioning yourself every time you look at something? I ask her, "What is your name?" It looks like I was living in a madhouse, as it were.

And then I couldn't contain the energy that was generating inside of me. Day after day, day after day, I felt that I couldn't possibly contain this, so I must do something about it. The next day S. was here, and I talked to him about this. He explained to me this is supposed to be the state of being that all the religious teachers have come into, and that I have come on the rivers there. And we all struggle, work hard, go to the temples for years and years and years, and I don't know what kind of special flowers you offered to God in your previous life…

Anyway, you have it and you must do something to control the escape of this energy out of your body. You come to India; we'll consult my father, as he is supposed to be an authority on yoga. Then I decided to go to India. But this continued for four or five months.

Q: In India?

U.G.: No, no. Here. But I was thoroughly and completely sick. I did nothing but rest inside. Then I went to India, and he suggested that I should go to a 48-day course of Yoga and breathing exercises. There was also some kind of a diet restriction: very bland food—milk and rice and some fruits and vegetables—for 48 days. They thought I would be able to control this. Not that "I" would be able to control this, but that somehow it would moderate the effects on the physical body.

Then he felt that I should go on for another 48 days. So I went on with the course, and it did help me to moderate the effects of these changes inside of me. I was still continuing the yoga. Now it was something very natural to me. There was no bewilderment. The awareness outside and the awareness inside. These are the two things that were there for me. When I looked at something there was no problem for me to ask what it was, but it had an effect on me.

Suddenly, somehow, the machinations of the mind or the mental activity came to an end without any volition or effort on my part. Then the body took over, as it were, and the senses became extraordinarily sensitive.

B: Is that still so?

U.G.: It is so. It is always so. What I am left with is only the body. There is nothing inside of me except the life—it's flowing to every part of the body. That is all.

B: So long as you use the word "I"...

U.G.: That is only a model for communication. I have to use the first-person singular. Not that there is the concept of the "I" all the time, but the whole structure has to come to an end because there is no such thing as a center in me at all. It's all the bodily reactions to the environment. I don't know if I have explained it? Maybe we can go into it and talk about it further. I don't know if I have communicated it.

B: How do you know when you're supposed to name a rose a "rose"? How will your mind begin to remember that it is necessary to even name a rose?

U.G.: It's a very simple process. I can now describe the process. Alright. You look at a flower. It is not that I am looking at a flower; the flower is looking at me. The flower is looking at me because of the eyes, you know? As long as the eyes are open they have to look at something or the other. If I close my eyes then there is no flower at all. There is a tree, there is a tree. But I don't look at it as a tree. The color is not there. If I use the word "object" the communication is very difficult. When you look at an object...if I use the world "object" it doesn't communicate exactly what it is there inside of me.

B: What happened? Did the object become you?

U.G.: No, no! The object doesn't become me.

B: But you say the word "object". Now, how to...?

U.G.: How do I communicate this to you? I see you.

B: Yes.

U.G.: I see her. These are two different things. How do I know that you are two different, that you are a woman, and that is a man? Because the light falls on you, your shape is different, your hair is different. The color of your clothes is different, and he has a different build, a different shape, and there is a space between you sitting and the sofa. Actually and factually, you are not different from the sofa. That's different.

Q: It is a description.

U.G.: No. There is nothing here. I am looking at all the things here. If I say that that is a chair, how do you distinguish the human being from the chair? Because you are all moving, obviously. You are animate things, and the others are inanimate things. Because the light is falling on you...on the retina, it is like a camera lens. If I turn this side you don't exist for me. What is there, the eyes look at. If I want to, if I know his name, I know who he is, and the whole thing, whatever I know is there in the background. The situation demands a need, whether this information can be of any value. So the moment I see he might not even recognize him. At the same time there are certain courtesies.

Q: Yes, quite.

U.G.: You know, common decency. We live in this world. The common decency suggests that I should say hello to him. You understand? The word is there for me to supply "Hello" or "Good morning." So each situation decides when and how the information that is there inside is necessary or is to be used. When that is over, I say "Hello" and there's some kind of a detaching. Then we are back again in the same way that I am looking at him, because there is a movement inside of him—the movement of life.

There is no thinking at all. At the very recognition of anything as an object or as a name thought comes in. So that means it is a waste of energy. The thought is a waste of energy. Ordinarily the thought does not come into my mind, into being, at all. And yet, there is already something that is going on because you are affecting me. Not that I am affecting you. If I see a thing, what you might call a beautiful rose, I don't call it a rose. I don't know that color is, right? I don't even call it a beautiful thing.

Maybe next to the rose are very deep yellow grass flowers. The eye automatically goes to them and not to this. Because the deep colors attract the eyes, and the retina captures that. The most beautiful flower has no importance. The deep yellow color of a grass flower makes the eyes go straight there. That may be why the mystics always talked about the dew drop on the grass because the reflection of the sun creates a very white color, and so the eye goes straight there. That attracts the eye.

It's not that "I" am looking at it. That has an effect. It has a physical effect on me. Because there is nobody else inside, there is no mental activity of any kind. Whatever you see is there in the environment—that affects the body. How do I know that affects the body?

If I take a walk from here to Gstaad, there is a very beautiful valley. I don't call it beautiful—I have no choice. So if there is a very picturesque landscape; we call it a picturesque landscape, I don't call it a picturesque landscape; the eyeballs become very fixed—they don't move. The beauty of that landscape, or whatever it is, immediately has a reaction on me, because I take a deep breath. You see? So it is a breath-taking view, otherwise why would I take a breath? So I walk a few steps further, I see a cow moving. I haven't called that a cow, a new-born baby. You look as if you have never looked at a cow—you see the waving of the tail and the moving head and horns.

Nothing is going on inside me; I am describing it in order to describe a state of being at that particular moment. Whatever the eyes see at that particular moment is all that is there for me in that world. That's all. There is nothing else. I move a little, and then I see something else coming. If there is anything beautiful around me it immediately has an effect on me.

So I breathe again and again and again, this living force goes on and on. And this breathing has an effect inside of me because the oxygen enters the cells in my body. The Hindus called them chakras, you know? You may have heard of them. The centers. I still have some of them. They appeared all over, the 34 spots that appeared on my body, wherever the chakras are supposed to be. They are not chakras, but the dormant glands that have suddenly become active. What activated this process is very difficult to know because when once the stepping-out process takes place, the triggering device is already there inside of you. It's automatic.

The triggering device, perhaps, has set in motion the whole process, particularly here. No, perhaps you can't see it. The lotus appeared on my forehead. This perhaps is the pineal gland, the pituitary gland or some gland, the new glands, all the dormant glands.

I became aware of this process because there are 64 parts on my body where I feel this pulse, not only here and here, but in 64 spots the throbbing of the life is felt by...I become aware, not "felt by somebody". When I breathe out the same process goes on, and the whole body heated up as a result of this breathing in and breathing out, and then it produces large quantities of saliva. The moment the saliva goes inside it generates electricity inside the body, and it goes on and on and on, whether you look at an object there or whether you listen to music.

No matter what I do, I have no choice. I can't say, "I'm going to listen to something", "I'm going to take a walk". When the body needs some exercise I take a walk. It's natural. So I usually take a walk. If I sit here and look out of the window, I can sit there and look out the window for the rest of my life. Because every time I look out I see something new which I have never seen before.

Every day I see this. Every automobile going there is a moving thing. I call it a "thing", but what is it? You always wonder about the "moving thing on the road." One after the other, one after the other, the automobiles come, different colors, different states, looking at them because there is nothing else to do.

For instance, I was told you were all coming here to talk at 3:45pm. If there is nothing there I go inside of my room and rest. When there is no awareness outside, there is an awareness inside. And what is that awareness inside me? You become aware of the whole movement of your body, the blood, the heartbeat. I listen to the heartbeat, you see? It's very interesting to listen to one's own heartbeat. There is all the time this tremendous...how shall I say it...this state of silence. Silence means not the absence of sound at all. The sounds are there, but there's no distinction. If somebody is playing a piano there or somebody is screaming noise from there, they are all the same. They come and hit you. That's all. The sound is there, and when you look at it the things are there.

And so I can stay in my bed. And there is no such thing as hunger for me because I feel when body needs food, and so I take food at regular intervals to keep the body going; otherwise I feel weak. For days and days I didn't take food at all, because there is no such thing as hunger at all. That seems to be the only thing that the body needs. What is left is only the body. The body has to be maintained in a perfect condition. It goes on and on and on and on, day after day. The first time you feel that, you feel that this is the way to live. The way the people live is something terrible because there are conflicts, contradictions. And why they worry themselves over all these things? This is the way to live. That is not the way to live.

Why do the people come with all kinds of questions? When I meet friends here, they come and ask thousands of questions. There are no questions for me at all. What happened is: we all are seeking something. It is not that you have arrived at a destination or that you have found what you have sought all your life but the structure suddenly comes to an end. That means there is no question inside of me. I am not only not questioning "What is this?", "What is that?", but also the so-called deeper problems. What is life? Is there any meaning in this world? In our existence does life have any purpose? How has this whole thing come into existence? All these questions are irrelevant. There is no questioner who is asking any questions of any kind anymore inside of me. Why do they ask all these questions?

Of course there are basic questions, if I don't know how to go to the railway station I will ask somebody. These are the questions of the day-to-day existence. But there is no questioner at all inside of me—no questioner asking questions of any kind anymore. The questioner has disappeared. Not that I have found the answers for all these questions. It's not a matter of saying that the metaphysical questions have no answers. It's not any of those things. It's just that the questioner has disappeared all of a sudden. By some luck, if you want to say, or by accident. How, I don't know.

After a point you can trace what happened, and then there is a leap. It is very difficult to describe how this leap happened and why it happened. What triggered the whole series of changes inside me? It's very difficult to find the missing link between the two. I can only say by some luck, or if you believe in some kind of grace....by grace of whom I wouldn't know at all. Somehow the whole thing happened and here I find myself, completely, a living human being living for the first time. For the first time the living quality inside of me has an opportunity to express itself in an extraordinarily sensitive way and is taking in everything that is there—whatever is present.

To be in this state of awareness is not in sense in which the psychologists use the word. Krishnamurti said he was in a state of choiceless awareness, but I have no choices of any kind. Whatever is present to me at that particular moment is all that is there for me. There is no need for me to close my eyes. As long as the eyes are open I see. The ears listen to the things. If I touch something, something is hot, something is soft, and then there's body consciousness even. So perhaps it's what the Hindus have called it, Sahaji Samadhi, a natural state.

Sometimes this goes into a different kind of state, as it were. Even the awareness disappears. That's the thing which I can't bring into being. It comes by itself, uninvited. I can't do a thing to bring that state into being. It's like saying to yourself, "I'm going to dream a beautiful dream." You can't do that. It comes all of a sudden from nowhere. The only thing that I feel is that something is descending upon me, filling my whole being, and it begins with this kind of peculiar feeling of the anesthetics. Suddenly the whole awareness disappears; the body becomes, for all practical purposes, dead, since it becomes very stiff. I prefer to lie down rather than sit at that time, and I prefer to close my eyes. I can keep my eyes open. Whether I keep my eyes open or closed it's no importance at all. All of it disappears from me. The eyes can be open and yet I see nothing. Nothing! Because there is no awareness feeling there. And then, sometimes, I know what happens. It begins here, and in the whole head a tightening process takes place. Then, some kind of a block. It's as if you are off completely.

Nothing exists for me. Even if I keep my eyes open they become bloodshot, as it were, and I can't see anything at all. I prefer to lie down during that period. Sometimes it lasts for half an hour, one hour, even two hours. If you look at the body it's like a stone. Can you tell me what happens to the body in that state? I don't know at all.

Q: It becomes almost very pale, yellowish, bluish. It's very much like a corpse. It definitely cannot last very long.

U.G.: Obviously, the signs of life are there. There's a heartbeat inside here, up to a point, as well as the pulse and the brainwaves.

Q: The breathing is very, very slow.

U.G.: The breathing becomes practically unnoticeable. When I come out suddenly then I realize that life is still there. And this sometimes happens two times, three times, four times. No one can say when this comes, why this comes or how this comes.

B: It is known in the investigation of the brain structure that it turns on something in the base of the brain, which can be affected by various chemicals.

U.G.: But what has happened to me? The brain that we have in common with the animals has undergone a radical change. You can very well ask me the question: how do I know? Because the billions of cells that we have in this brain. They say that we have 10 billion cells, and then 100 billion other connecting cells.

The cells inside the bone also underwent a radical mutation, if I may use that word. Because when there is a change in the cell, when there is a sudden lack of the center, the "I", or whatever you call it, this body has to undergo a transformation.

Every gland in my body, every cell in my body, has undergone a radical mutation. Why do I use the word mutation? Because I can't think of a more appropriate word. Every cell in my body has undergone a transformation. Every gland has undergone a transformation because it seems to be functioning in a different way. The brain waves are incredible, and I would very much like to have the opportunity to use a brain wave machine. The electricity that goes out of my body is tremendous since there is no point inside of me. There is no space for me at all.

If I close my eyes...I tried all this. I am very skeptical of this whole business. Anyway, that is why perhaps they have used the word enlightenment or illumination. Even when I close my eyes there is light here. The whole thing is filled with light. There is no body at all. There is nobody consciousness whether I keep my eyes open or closed. It doesn't make any difference. I can look at this hand, and if I call it a hand, then "Whose hand is it?" is the next question.

There is no awareness of the body at all. There is no body at all. This I experiment with. The light penetrates through the eyelids, you know? When you close your eyes there is a hole here; some kind of a third eye, or whatever you want to call it. I padded these eyes with thick cloths, and still there was light inside, because there is some kind of a hole here inside. The light penetrates through that, and the body is filled with this light. There is light inside. That's perhaps the reason why they call it enlightenment or illumination.

Then it expands. The electricity that is generated in this body goes to the end of the universe, affecting the whole thing. When I come out of this state, whatever you call it, the whole body is filled with peace. It's some kind of a substance, like a white substance. The whole body is filled with this white substance. You can look at it and it shines like a phosphorescence. It's the whole body. What this process is I don't know.

I'm not interested in even finding out what this is. One of these days, perhaps, they will find out; the medical technology will discover the dormant glands inside the body. They say that we have so many glands inside the intestines. They don't know why they are there or what functions they perform. They really don't know. Perhaps one of these days they will go into the whole thing and find out. What I am left with, if I may put it that way, is the pure and simple physical being.

But yet, this body is a different body. There is a consciousness that is operating, if I may use that word. After all, there is no difference between life and consciousness. Life is consciousness, consciousness is life. If you say consciousness of a different quality, that is all very fine. But the next question is...

I have no questions at all. No questions at all. I don't know if human evolution has any purpose at all. If it has any purpose this seems to be the end-product of the human evolution. This mutation has changed the whole animalistic content of the brain, especially the part of the brain which is common with the animal. This may be the reason, the cause. For the first time, somehow, you have flowered into a real human being. The possibility of the human evolution flowering into a human being is there. That is all that I am going to stress. There is a state of being.

This was my fundamental question. I started very early when I was 14. What is there beneath and behind all the religious concepts we have in this world today? Is there anything at all? The people who were around me were thoughts—all mental experiences. It's within the field of thought. I myself went through the various kinds of mental experiences within the field the thought.

Except for perhaps one person, whom I met: Ramana Maharishi, not Mahesh Maharishi of Beatles fame. He was living in a small village. Somehow I felt that he had this, but it was my assumption.

And the second one I met, naturally, was J. Krishnamurti. But I have always had this nagging doubt about the chap. You see, I hammered him day after day for weeks. "What is it that you have? Do you have anything at all? I'm not interested in the abstractions you are throwing at me." I know all this because I have been through the mill, and I know every bit of it. I have studied psychology. I know all that. I'm not interested in your abstractions, you see? This, any intelligent man can do. But what is there? Is there anything at all? That is my question. It doesn't matter to me if he has it or if he hasn't. That is no more a question for me. But is it the same? I really don't know. Perhaps it is the same.

I can't be different—what is there behind it. There is no comparative thing inside of me. These questions don't interest me at all—whether he has it or not? This must be the basis because of a religious experience. Experience is a very trivial thing. The mind can experience the many states of experiencing. But this is something beyond thought. This is the thing which thought can never penetrate. In that state, where this action takes place, I have no way of knowing what is happening. But yet there seems to be some kind of an awareness.

There is a difference between sleep and this state. Something is aware of something else. The Hindu religious thinkers said the immensity is aware of its own immensity, or *that* is aware of *that*. I have posed that life is aware of itself. Something is there. But the thought can never penetrate and tell what it is.

When I come out of it there is a tremendous state of relaxation. The whole body is in a state of relaxation, which you can call love, bliss, truth, God, reality, or anything you like, but it is not that, because there is nobody who is looking at it. I can bring out the word and say that this is a microphone. I can look at it and say what is there, the awareness inside of me. How the air is moving inside of me. But this thing I have no way of finding a word to communicate and tell you what that is. If I use the word bliss, it is not bliss! Perhaps it is bliss. What is it? I have no word at all to describe that.

To use any of these words—love, truth, God, reality or anything—is not right. They are inadequate words to express a state of being which is beyond words. There is no way to describe that state of being. In that state something happens. What happens is you are dead and are born again. There is no difference between life and death at all. The continuity is gone once and for all. The whole slate is wiped out and it is clean.

The next thing is it writes itself again, and then it wipes itself. There is only one memory, and that records there. If there is any use for it it comes, otherwise there is no use. I read the Time magazine. Every phrase is implanted in that. I don't take any position when I'm reading. I just read it to keep myself aware with what is happening in the field of human thought, and also in the world.

Yesterday I was reading a science article. All these phrases come when there is a need for me to express something. The phrases are ready, supplied. The information is there, ready. The whole encyclopedic knowledge that I have acquired is there in the background, but only if there is a need. See? Who is to decide the need? I have a difficulty now to describe this. It's very difficult for me to look at that and describe it. To describe this state is very difficult because there is always a gap. It's not that I am struggling or that somebody is trying to bring it out. The words have to come out in their own way. To describe the awareness inside of me at this particular moment: that seems to be...

B: Are you aware of time?

U.G.: Time. There is no time. There is no space. These are bored statements because the thought is time. There is thought—there is time. As long as I am aware of the things outside there is a space. I am looking at the things—they are space in their own way. Because I have restored vision now I see much more—my eyes take in completely 100%. They say that the eye cuts out 98% and lets in only 2%. But now, since there is no choice of any kind, it takes in the whole thing, and I have a complete vision. But not behind. If I want to look I have to turn the whole body. This is the only time when I am aware this. Not that I am aware of this state. There is a state of and by itself. It's not because there is somebody who is looking at it.

If I close my eyes there is no space at all because there is no center here at all. The delight is part of the whole space. To say that I am the space is not correct. The light inside has no frontiers. I want to explain this simile.

I explained it to you the other day. This is the social consciousness, the mind, the whole world. This is the enclosure, the "I" which I have built through...

Q: Generations.

U.G.: Not generations, but at least from the beginning. Like a baby you say, "This is a microphone." And the next time you see it you repeat it and say, "This is a microphone." That is all. The word structure is built up. Every cell carries the accumulate knowledge of generations, 14 millions years of thought that is there in this individual. This "I" is a very difficult thing to break, if you lose one brick you immediately put plaster and you close it. This is actually not different. The human mind, or the human consciousness, or whatever you call it, is not different from the social consciousness.

Somehow, by some process, this knocks itself off. I can't do it. The more thought I put into this, the more methods I use, the more difficult it becomes. Because this is a strengthening factor. If somehow this structure collapses, once and for all, what is here is outside. But this explosion is not an ordinary thing. It is something like a nuclear explosion. It's of a terrific nature. When this explosion takes place, naturally, the whole human consciousness, as a whole, is affected by this.

You may very well ask me: why do you make such a bold statement? It's a series of explosions every now and then that are taking place, and then the fallout affects the human consciousness. This seems to be the only way we can affect the world: by bringing about a structural change within oneself. Not through any other process you are going to change the world at all. Even this is going to be a very microscopic effect on the world.

To say that I am this space is an absurd thing. It seems that there is no separation between the things; whether I keep my eyes open or closed is immaterial. What is the difference? Because these are two holes here looking at what? But what if there is a need for me to go to the Gstaad Palace Hotel? If I want to go there I know. It's not as if I don't know. Why do you want to go? What purpose? These are all of no importance at all.

The thinker has no existence at all. It is an artificially created thinker. He has taken possession of the body, and has dominated for years and years and years. He is not there anymore. And what we are left with is this and the thought. How do you become aware of the thoughts? What is thought?

As long as the thinker is there is it possible for you to look at the thought? Impossible! Because the thought splits itself into two—one thought is looking at the other—one image looking at the other. There is no way of looking at your thought—it is impossible. Only when you step outside the whole structure of individual consciousness, social consciousness, there is a possibility of finding out how the thought originates in you.

Thought is very simple because it has no content. Thought has been part of the human consciousness right from the very beginning. You can't trace the origin. Perhaps that's the reason why you have the statement in the Bible: "In the beginning was the Word, and the word was the flesh." So it is matter. And at the same time it is sound.

The thought comes. Why it comes you don't know. The thought sometimes comes. It's like an electronic eye: when the thought comes the awareness is disturbed—you become aware of the thoughts. This very awareness destroys that thought. Thought takes root there and brings the thinker in. The situation decides how long and what part of the thought is necessary.

Thought is a word, and word is a sound. So this sound has been in existence through centuries. Thought is of no importance at all. Thought has no importance at all anymore. When there is a need, when there is a necessity for the thought it is there. It is not that I am thoughtless.

When the thoughts come in there is nobody who says this is right, this is wrong, this is a pleasant thought, that is an unpleasant thought. There is nobody who is saying that, you see? So it is of no importance. If thoughts or the feelings come, they hit me here, in the heart. There are all kinds of feelings. And what that particular feeling is, there is nobody to say this is a sex feeling, this is a feeling of irritation, this is a feeling of jealousy or envy. All these are not there.

One after the other they hit you. You look at a flower there and that hits you. You look at a moving car; that hits you. You look at an animal there; that hits you. You look at what you call a beautiful place; that hits you. And so you don't know what they are; they are just one after the other, one after the other, the molecular bombardment.

The whole thing is vibrating with all these vibrations that come from the outside. There are vibrations. As you go along all these vibrations and feelings (what we call feelings) have no importance at all. Sometimes the thought comes, and the awareness is like a searchlight. As it is arising, it is destroying.

Sometimes these old memories of mine come. You become aware of that. This is a nasty thought you had towards some individual, and so when it enters the awareness, the brain cells become so tight here. The words come here and go away, but this whole tightening process takes place inside the head, and it has no place anymore to take its roots. It's gone. The thoughts come and go.

Sometimes there are no thoughts. It's like the electronic eye. They come, and the moment they come—it's a simultaneous process—the awareness also does. It is a quick process. But it is of no importance at all.

B: That may be the main point because a thought coming in which disturbs the mind. We could discuss the question of the root of thought. You say you don't know but...

U.G.: I don't put that question to myself because if I put any question, at first I start with a state of not knowing. I really don't know any question.

If you ask me "What is mind?"; for me to get on a platform and talk about mind is one of the most absurd things because what is mind? Why do you want to ask the question "what is mind"?

Then the exploration begins. What is the exploration? The thinker has to come in. The thought process develops—what is the mental activity? It's not mind. For all practical purposes the mental activity is the mind. Alright. When the mental activity comes to an end that is one of the most extraordinary experiences. If you can experience that, the quieting of the mental activity, the quiet mind.

The experience of a silent mind. That changes the whole process of thinking. That is how all the conversions have taken place, the mystical experiences, or even the scientific experiences. It is still within the field of thought.

For instance, it would be impertinent for me to talk of Einstein. I did physics for my basic degree. For so long we were all caught up in the Newtonian physics, nobody could break through. Einstein, somehow, by some process, realized the inadequacy of Newtonian thought and that itself acted as a breakthrough. Now we connect them. Without Newtonian physics Einstein would never have come into existence at all. As a flashback you see this. But there at that particular point the mental activity had come to an end—but not actually.

Again, it caught that experience and created the thought structure. So this revolution is within the structure of thought. Any such revolution within the structure of thought is a revolution in itself, but the thought structure is still there. It brings about a change in character, like in all the conversions we have in the history of mystics in Europe.

I forget her name, but there was a prostitute, to whom suddenly this mystical experience happened. She wrote books and poems in the language of the streets, which was the basis and inspiration of Dante. So it was within the field of thought. The mystical experience, all religious experience, all the experience within the field of thought changes the individual consciousness. From that moment on your way of looking at things is as if you have new glasses. Everything you look at is different. Every activity of yours is different. Every movement of your thought is different. It has undergone a change, a radical change, but still within the field of thought.

Bringing the mental activity to some kind of a silence is not the end of it. That itself can perform a miracle. That is the first loosening of the whole process of this structure. Then the memory of the brain cells, every cell has a memory of its own. The whole human body has to change. You have to become silent. In this case the whole thing is silent. Every thought, every brain cell, all the 10 hundred billion cells—they become silent. There is a tremendous silence.

This silence is of a different quality and a different kind. It's not of the mind at all; not within the field of thought. As you go on and on and on you come to a point where you will not be able to differentiate between the human mind and the world. They are one and the same—they are not two different things. But for purposes of convenience we have created this enclosure, and we have a feeling that we are individuals. We are not actually individuals.

Somehow the whole structure collapses. The individualization takes place. You become an individual. That means you have become a flower. Since there is no thought structure anymore there is no "I" anymore. What it is left with is the body. What is inside the body? This life.

This life is not different from the creative life. This is the creative energy. You can say all these words but talking about the creative energy that has created the whole universe is going into the field of mysticism, and so it doesn't mean a thing at all.

So I come back to the same point, after exploring all this, I come to the same point and ask myself the question: What is mind? I have no answer. There is no question—the question has disappeared in the process. So answering the question seems to me of no importance at all.

The origin of the thought is the thing which you don't know at all. You don't know at all. Somehow it's there. That is a part of the consciousness inside, the life itself. The brain mechanism seems to have this spark of being. I can't really give a satisfactory answer to that.

B: I really meant not the origin of thought, but the question of what is the origin of the continuity of thought?

U.G.: There is no continuity.

B: You say that the awareness wipes out thought when it starts, but if it doesn't wipe out thought...

U.G.: That means the "I" is there. If the "I" is there he carries on. He wants more and more and more and more thought. Since now this thought is incapable of bringing the thinker into existence. You understand? Before that happens this thought disappears. It's like those doors you have in the airports—the moment you set your foot down the door opens—the thought comes. There is a break in your awareness because of the thought. The thought is there and it's not there the next moment. It has no chance to bring the thinker into operation at all. The continuity is lost. There is no continuity any more. I recognize this as a microphone and the purpose and all of that. The next time, I have to do it again.

B: If you want to communicate, which you seem to want to do…

U.G.: That's not part of my problems. I may not even want to but I am beginning to feel that even without communicating there is a possibility of being silent in some corner. There is nobody deluding oneself because this fallout perhaps will affect in its own way. I don't know. I really don't know.

Another difficulty for me is the mode of expression. I have no way of expressing myself. The whole past is wiped out. And that past included Krishnamurti too. The Krishnamurtian lingo, if I may use that word, is of no value at all to me. I can't use that at all. It's impossible for me. I don't even know what he's talking now except for a few phrases. The easy thing for an individual is to fall back on that lingo.

With all the religious teachers, the literature was there, they used "God", they used all the expressions. This man somehow has developed a new mode of expression. To me that seems inadequate. Perhaps it helps others—I don't know—I can't say anything about others.

The break between Newton and Einstein…The Newtonian physics had to come to a stop within me. The whole structure has collapsed, and that structure included Krishnamurti. I can't use any of those things. How am I going to create new words? I can't create new words at all, because I have to use the inadequate words that we have.